MAKING
FREE TRADE
WORK

Other publications from the Council's International Trade Project

After Reagan:
Confronting the Changed World Economy
C. Michael Aho and Marc Levinson
Council on Foreign Relations (1988)

Bilateralism, Multilateralism and Canada in U.S. Trade Policy
William Diebold, Jr., editor
Ballinger Publishing, Inc. (1988)

Fixing Farm Trade:
Policy Options for the United States
Robert L. Paarlberg
Ballinger Publishing, Inc. (1987)

Trade Talks: America Better Listen!
C. Michael Aho and Jonathan D. Aronson
Council on Foreign Relations (1985, 1987)

MAKING FREE TRADE WORK

The Canada–U.S. Agreement

Peter Morici, editor

Council on Foreign Relations Press
New York • London

COUNCIL ON FOREIGN RELATIONS BOOKS

The Council on Foreign Relations, Inc., is a nonprofit and non-partisan organization devoted to promoting improved understanding of international affairs through the free exchange of ideas. The Council does not take any position on questions of foreign policy and has no affiliation with, and receives no funding from, the United States government.

From time to time, books and monographs written by members of the Council's research staff or visiting fellows, or commissioned by the Council, or written by an independent author with critical review contributed by a Council study or working group are published with the designation "Council on Foreign Relations Book." Any book or monograph bearing that designation is, in the judgement of the Committee on Studies of the Council's board of directors, a responsible treatment of a significant international topic worthy of presentation to the public. All statements of fact and expressions of opinion contained in Council books are, however, the sole responsibility of the author.

Copyright 1990 by the Council on Foreign Relations, Inc.
All rights reserved.
Printed in the United States of America

This book may not be reproduced, in whole or in part, in any form (beyond that copying permitted by Sections 107 and 108 of the U.S. Copyright Law and excerpts by reviewers for the public press), without written permission from the publishers. For information, write Publications Office, Council on Foreign Relations, 58 East 68th Street, New York, NY 10021.

Library of Congress Cataloguing-in-Publication Data

Making free trade work : the Canada–U.S. agreement / Peter Morici, editor.
    p.   cm.—(The Council on Foreign Relations series on international trade)
    Includes bibliographical references.
    ISBN 0-87609-078-1
    1. Canada. Treaties, etc. United States, 1988 Jan. 2.
2. Tariff—Law and legislation—United States.   3. Free trade—
United States.   4. Tariff—Law and legislation—Canada.   5. Free
trade—Canada.   I. Morici, Peter.   II. Series.
KF6668.C321988M35   1990
343.7305′6′0971–dc20
[347.303560971]
                                     89-71317
                                        CIP

90   91   92   93   94   95   96   PB   9   8   7   6   5   4   3   2   1   0

CONTENTS

FOREWORD

C. Michael Aho

The ratification of the Canada–U.S. Free Trade Agreement (FTA) in January 1989 was a historic event, but it was not the end of the process; it marked only the beginning of a long and uncharted road of implementation and evolution. Even at 1,000 pages plus, the agreement is not a complete document. Much work remains to be done, negotiations will continue, and the future is littered with potential stumbling blocks. The success of the agreement will depend critically upon how the two countries behave in response to changing circumstances.

The agreement is unprecedented both for Canada and the United States. Canada had flirted with the idea of a bilateral free trade agreement with its southern neighbor for over 100 years, but each time it backed down for fear of being overwhelmed economically, politically, and culturally by a country ten times its size. Indeed, even on this occasion, the Free Trade Agreement became the single issue of a hard-fought campaign in the Canadian national election, with Prime Minister Brian Mulroney's Conservative Party, which negotiated the agreement, winning by a narrow margin.

For the United States, too, bilateral free trade is unprecedented. U.S. trade policy previously had been focused almost entirely on the multilateral negotiations held under the auspices of the General Agreement on Tariffs and Trade (GATT). Increasingly frustrated with that process, the Reagan administration turned to a "bilateral option." A limited free trade agreement was signed with Israel in 1985. In that same year, the far reaching negotiations with Canada were begun. The Reagan administration deserves credit for successfully negotiating the pact with Canada, because it did signal that trade liberalization is still possible and that international trade negotiations can still bear fruit.

The Canada–U.S. Free Trade Agreement has gone further, faster than the current round of multilateral trade negotiations being held under the GATT—the so-called Uruguay Round—and could, in fact, act as a catalyst to those talks. The FTA covered virtually all the same items on the Uruguay Round agenda, including most of the new issues: services and investment, but not intellectual property. Riding high on the success of the Canada–U.S. agreement, there is now talk of the United States negotiating other bilaterals.

Before going full speed ahead with the bilateral option, the United States should stand back and take stock of this agreement with Canada. This volume is an attempt to do just that. The FTA is a complex, comprehensive agreement that was complicated to negotiate despite the vast similarities in both countries' legal and business environments. Significant gaps on subsidies, services, and intellectual property remain. And the institutional foundation of the agreement has yet to be tested.

In the introductory chapter, Peter Morici describes the terms of the agreement, as well as the overall economic environment within which the agreement must be implemented. He raises numerous questions, including: How will the agreement evolve—with time and with changing international, and domestic, circumstances? How will both countries behave in response to Europe 1992, or to prolonged disagreement on agriculture trade? A common position may be possible on Europe 1992, but will the United States and Canada share a common interest in cutting a deal with the Community on agriculture? How will the bilateral blend with the multilateral talks, and will Canada seek to recontract if the United States extends similar privileges to other countries during the Uruguay Round?

Regarding the terms of the agreement itself, how durable will it be? This will depend, in part, on the first major tests of the dispute settlement process and, in part, on the pressures for protection that would emanate from an economic downturn. And, how and when will the gaps in the agreement be filled in, for example, on specific service sectors and on developing common laws on subsidies?

Since the agreement was literally unprecedented, there are no precedents to build upon. As a result, the implementation process is likely to be just as challenging as the negotiations themselves, as well as frustrating and fraught with frictions. David Leyton-Brown lays out the potential stumbling blocks and raises questions on how both countries will behave as events unfold, particularly with respect to the elaborate institutional architecture. A primary focus of his political analysis is the asymmetry of interests between the two countries. Given that the Canadian election was fought over the proposed agreement, Canadian citizens had a steady diet of news and opinions. Even today, Canadian newspapers are rife with articles on the agreement. In contrast, in the United States, interest peaked—but it was never very high—when the negotiation was completed. Will the United States hold up its side of the bargain? Leyton-Brown makes specific suggestions—to Canadian and American policymakers, as well as to the private sectors in both countries—to shore up interest in making free trade work.

With the trade barriers falling, the labor force in both countries will have to make adjustments. How will the agreement affect workers, and are the safeguards—that are necessary for political acceptability in both countries—adequate? J. David Richardson examines the likely consequences for worker displacements and adjustments. He proposes new programs for workers and small firms that could be adopted in the ongoing negotiations to fill in the gaps. Given the widespread restructuring that could occur as Canada and the United States achieve a truly integrated single market, such a proposal may need to be adopted, particularly in Canada.

The most contentious issue during the negotiation—in fact it almost derailed the talks in the eleventh hour—was the attempt to develop common rules covering subsidies. The basic question was, and still is, what policies are fair and which are unfair? Because the Canadian and American negotiators could not agree, they set up an elaborate binational dispute settlement process, and called for ongoing negotiations (for five to seven years) to try to develop common rules. Gary Horlick and Debra Steger assess the possibilities of developing a common set of rules in subsequent negotiations, and assess the linkages to the Uruguay Round negotiations on subsidies. Can serious negotiations on subsidies begin before the conclusion of the Uruguay Round? Or, will Canada or the United States, or both, prefer to wait until those talks are completed? Since both Horlick and Steger had privileged access to the subsidies discussions during the original negotiations, their insights into the complexities of the issue, and their suggestions for bridging the differences of opinion between the two countries, could help to stimulate a successful outcome.

One of the most vexing questions raised by bilateral agreements is: What are the effects on third countries? Sidney Weintraub in his chapter focuses upon the impact on the most significant third party in this instance, Mexico. Weintraub explores what circumstances would pressure Mexico into seeking its own bilateral agreement with the United States and, perhaps, Canada. In a disaggregation of Canadian and Mexican exports to the United States, Weintraub illustrates that there is a significant overlap, particularly in autos and auto parts, energy, petrochemicals, and agriculture. In 1989, the United States and Mexico signed a framework agreement and, today, there is talk of going beyond that with sectoral agreements. But if the United States and Mexico want to strike a deal on trade in automobiles, Canada would certainly have something to say about it. There will be no escaping these issues when the United States and Mexico ultimately sit down to negotiate.

In the penultimate chapter, Peter Morici assesses the impact of bilateral initiatives on future U.S. trade policy, and on the trading system as a whole. The significance of the Canada–U.S. agreement should not be underestimated, especially since it marks a departure in U.S. trade policy.

Here I would like to add a few personal observations on how future bilateral initiatives by the United States could affect the overall trading system. The Canada–U.S agreement is a good agreement, but it did not address many of the central difficulties of trade between the two countries, such as subsidies, trade remedy actions, government procurement, and intellectual property. The FTA took almost two years to negotiate, and the talks came perilously close to collapsing on several occasions. Before launching another bilateral, would it not be better to wait and see how this one works out? Furthermore, additional bilateral agreements may create more problems than they resolve.

Bilateral free trade agreements are justified only in special cases. Israel, for political reasons, and Canada, for reasons of proximity and interdependence, are special cases. The European Community is also a special case on the latter score. President Reagan in his 1988 State of the Union address spoke of including Mexico in a North American accord. Mexico, for reasons that range from debt to demography to drugs, may also be a special case. But after Mexico, it is hard to envision other countries or the private sector in the United States going along with any other bilateral agreements.

To put it more bluntly, a succession of bilateral trade agreements is a recipe for RIBS—resentment, inefficiency, bureaucracy, and silly signals. Resentment would prevail among outsiders. Inefficiency would be spawned by the fragmentation of markets. Bureaucratic nightmares would result for governments and private firms trying to cope with the discrimination among countries. And silly signals would be sent to those policymakers in developing countries who are proponents of markets and multilateralism. Lastly, other countries would protest if the United States tried to go beyond these special cases.

A proliferation of bilateral agreements is inconsistent with an expanding trading system. History can be instructive here; lessons can be learned from the 1930s. In the wake of the Smoot-Hawley tariff and subsequent retaliation, many countries tried to establish bilateral or regional agreements in an attempt to gain some predictability for trade. But because the bilateral agreements were largely discriminatory, the predictability gained was illusory: the conclusion of the second or third discriminatory agreement necessarily disappoints expectations created by the first. Frictions, if not downright hostility, are bound to arise amongst the parties to the agreements. The lesson to be learned is: if other countries follow the U.S. lead by trying to negotiate bilateral agreements that offer mutually incompatible privileges, then predictability and stability would be destroyed for all.

The arguments against a series of bilaterals are as much political ones, as they are economic. Bilateralism is, in essence, to play favorites; this creates foreign policy problems with those that are discriminated against. In addition, if a misguided bilateral strategy is pursued, the political contours of the Western Alliance could be altered. Domestic political problems will crop up as well. If a country is deemed to be acting inconsistently with U.S. foreign policy objectives, or if important domestic sectors are suffering increased competition from a particular country, Congress will be under pressure to withdraw trade preferences or withhold further liberalization. Do members of Congress want to get involved in such micromanagement of trade and foreign policy initiatives? Does Congress have the time, resources, or political will to review, oversee, and legislate a series of bilaterals with all of the attendant political pressures that they entail?

Given the manifold drawbacks of further bilateral deals, the United States must stick with the multilateral process. If it falters, the United States should not give up; it should unilaterally pressure other countries to pick up the pieces and move on in the multilateral forum. Here, the bilateral option can be useful as a threat. But the threat must be credible, in that the administration and Congress must be willing to carry it out. If the administration is serious about threatening further bilaterals, it should continue to explore the option with Mexico and weigh the costs and consequences such an agreement would entail. Meanwhile, the administration should push hard on the multilateral negotiations, using Mexico as the credible threat. Besides, could the United States really contemplate giving preferential access to other major trading partners while denying it to Mexico?

In the meantime, the United States should pay close attention to the Canadian pact, because if this bilateral deal should fall by the wayside, the credibility of the bilateral threat will be undermined; this would, in turn, slow progress in the multilateral negotiations. The footdraggers in those negotiations will argue, "See, even the United States and Canada, with their strong trade ties and similar business environments, could not agree on these sensitive issues." Peter Morici, in the concluding chapter, provides several suggestions to prevent this from happening.

The chapters in this volume were presented to a Council on Foreign Relations study group that met five times between October 1988 and 1989. (The study group members are listed in the Appendix.) The finished product—*Making Free Trade Work*—is one of a series of books produced by the Council on Foreign Relations' International Trade Project. It is the second book on U.S.–Canada trade relations. The first, *Bilateralism, Multilateralism and Canada in U.S. Trade Policy*, edited by William Diebold, Jr., was released in the spring of 1988. Other books produced by the Project include *Trade Talks: America Better Listen!*, by Aho and Aronson (1987), *Fixing Farm Trade*, by Paarlberg (1988), and *After Reagan: Confronting the Changed World Economy*, by Aho and Levinson (1988). *Governments and Corporations in a Shrinking World: Trade and Innovation Policies in the United States, Europe, and Japan*, by Sylvia Ostry, the 1988–1989 Volvo Distinguished Visiting Fellow at the Council on Foreign Relations, was published in the spring of 1990. Future volumes will focus on international corporate alliances, the challenges and consequences of European integration, trade problems in high-technology industries, and U.S. trade policy after the Uruguay Round. In all, the Project will produce a dozen monographs, all based upon Council study groups.

The Council would like to thank the Ford Foundation for its generous funding of this study, and General Motors and the Rockefeller Foundation for their generous funding of the International Trade Project. I would also like to thank Bill Diebold who so ably chaired the study group, and the members of the Project's Steering Committee (see Appendix) chaired by Edmund T. Pratt, Jr. I am also grateful to Peter Tarnoff, president of the Council, and Nicholas Rizopoulos, vice president for studies, for their unwavering support. Alison von Klemperer, assistant director of the Trade Project, Suzanne Hooper, managing editor of the publications program, and Dorothy Price are due accolades for coordinating the study group and producing the volume. Finally, I would heartily like to thank Peter Morici, who did a superb job selecting the contributors to this volume, editing their work, and delivering the finished manuscript punctually.

C. Michael Aho is director of the International Trade Project and director of economic studies at the Council on Foreign Relations.

MAKING
FREE TRADE
WORK

1

THE ENVIRONMENT FOR FREE TRADE

Peter Morici

The Canada–U.S. Free Trade Agreement (FTA) is one of the most ambitious agreements establishing a free trade area under the General Agreement on Tariffs and Trade (GATT). By eliminating tariffs and most import and export measures, the FTA ensures that most of the benefits of duty-free trade in goods will be achieved by the end of the 1990s. With regard to most nontariff barriers and services, the FTA establishes a standstill on new discriminatory practices and promises continuing progress through negotiations. The two governments have assigned high priority to formulating new, joint rules governing domestic subsidies and dumping. In addition, the agreement enshrines recently liberalized rules for direct investment flows.

The United States and Canada conceived and are implementing the FTA in a period of rapid change in the broader international economy and of stress in the multilateral trading system. Adjustments imposed by the FTA—both on business and labor from increased specialization and on governmental and political structures from the agreement's constraints on domestic policies and practices—come on top of more far-reaching changes being imposed by the global economy.

The focus on nontariff measures as well as tariffs, on services and investment as well as goods, makes the FTA, its effective implementation, and the pursuit of follow-on negotiations difficult and complex. The FTA is not a done deal—it is a dynamic agreement requiring major commitments of bureaucratic and political resources to live up to its full potential. The benefits each country receives from the FTA will be strongly determined by how effectively the measures already agreed to are implemented; the success of follow-on negotiations; and how

1

the two countries respond to new challenges in the multilateral environment. This volume, which is an outgrowth of a Council on Foreign Relations study group on the future of the FTA, addresses important aspects of these issues.

TRENDS IN THE INTERNATIONAL ECONOMY

Canada's motivations for entering into the agreement, despite its historical ambivalence about such an arrangement, have important origins in the challenges that country faces in adjusting to global competition. Specifically, most economists and policymakers anticipate that free trade with the United States will help improve the productivity of Canada's underspecialized manufacturing sector. For the United States, the FTA is perceived as part of a broader, multilateral trade strategy. Economic changes at home and abroad have constrained U.S. exports in areas of traditional strength—agriculture, high technology, and services—and thus have made the discipline of foreign practices that impede market access more critical to U.S. interests. In the United States, policymakers saw a trade agreement with Canada as a means for stimulating broader, multilateral progress with regard to these practices, as well as for addressing important issues in the bilateral relationship with Canada.

The following discussion examines key trends in the international economic system that are inducing adjustments and motivating policymakers in both countries, and analyzes some of the issues and problems these trends are likely to create in the bilateral relationship and the FTA. The next section of this essay briefly reviews the Canadian and U.S. objectives in negotiating the FTA and the essential elements of the agreement. Drawing on this background, the concluding section pulls together key issues that subsequent chapters address in detail.

The United States in the Global Economy

During the 1970s, as U.S. competitiveness waned in a succession of mature industries—such as textiles and steel—and the cost of energy imports rose, a view emerged among policymakers and economists that the United States could pay for rising imports by emphasizing its comparative advantages in agriculture, high-technology manufacturing, and services. Structural factors—notably, shifts in comparative advantages, discussed here, and macroeconomic constraints, addressed below—have made these kinds of adjustments more difficult than envisioned.

In *agriculture,* technological breakthroughs and more market-responsive policies have increased productivity in some middle-income developing countries—as Brazil, India, and Indonesia, for example—and in China. As a result, growth in the demand for exports from the United States, Canada, and the European Community (EC) has been limited. These trends—along with an overvalued dollar from 1982 to 1985; U.S. farm support programs that raised commodity prices above world levels; and protectionist practices in the EC, Japan, and elsewhere—cut the share of agricultural products in U.S. exports from 19 percent in 1981 to 12 percent in 1988.

In *high-technology manufacturing,* such as commercial aviation and advanced electronics, the United States faces escalating competition from Japan and some countries in Western Europe. These developments are firmly rooted in a general evening of research and development (R&D) efforts and technological capabilities among the major advanced industrial countries, and in a greater emphasis among U.S. competitors on civilian and privately financed R&D than is present in the United States. Also important is the aggressive use abroad of industrial and trade policies intended to improve competitive performance vis-à-vis U.S. firms.[1]

Over the last two decades, the contributions of *services*—that is, travel, transportation, fees and royalties, and private business services—to U.S. exports have not shown the dramatic growth once anticipated.[2] Many service exports have been constrained by a maze of foreign practices lying outside the jurisdiction of the GATT; these are on the Uruguay Round agenda, but progress will be slow. Equally significant, many factors contributing to competitiveness in high-technology manufacturing—namely, investments in R&D and a highly trained labor force—are important in business services. As the experience and education of the labor force in Japan and the newly industrializing countries

(NICs) improve and these countries' achievements in technology-intensive manufacturing grow, the United States will encounter even greater competition.[3]

What does this portend for the structure of the U.S. economy? The U.S. economy is likely to be more balanced in the 1990s than was anticipated ten or fifteen years ago. Weakened comparative advantages in agriculture and knowledge-intensive industries imply improved competitiveness elsewhere. We should expect a greater market-induced role for import-competing, domestic producers in mature industries, such as automotive products and textiles; however, labor adjustment pressures will continue, and not all industries and communities will fare equally well.

Particularly important in the context of U.S.–Canadian trade are prospects for the nonferrous metals and steel industry. Synthetic materials and advances in electronics have substantially reduced the demand for copper, lead, zinc, and most other nonferrous metals, as well as steel. The downsizing of cars has had the same general consequences for steel and some nonferrous metals.[4]

The decline in the exchange rate for the dollar from 1985 to 1988 and the length of the current economic expansion have helped improve the sales and profitability of domestic producers in many mature industries. However, in virtually all of manufacturing, employment growth has been, and will remain, slow or negative as new industrial technologies continue to spread.[5] The longer-term prospects for growth in domestic demand for steel and most nonferrous metals remain severely limited.

The estimates David Richardson summarizes in chapter 3 indicate that the basic U.S. nonferrous metals industry could face significant employment losses as a result of FTA tariff cuts. During the next recession, the superior competitive position of Canadian producers could cause U.S. producers to seek relief under the FTA bilateral safeguard provisions or broader remedies that may be obtained under U.S. trade law. The latter would test the agreement's ability to shield effectively an important Canadian industry from U.S. contingent protection.

With regard to steel, the Canadian industry has the competitive potential to increase its penetration into the U.S. market. Its market share is currently constrained by informal participation in the U.S. program of voluntary restraint agreements (VRAs). Steel VRAs are likely to continue. If the Canadian industry ceased limiting exports, then either the U.S. industry would face yet another source of adjustment pressures or the market shares of other foreign suppliers would have to be further reduced. The latter scenario highlights the potential consequences of preferential market access for Canadian suppliers under the FTA when the United States seeks to protect distressed industries. In chapter 6, I discuss this issue further in the context of the FTA's third-country effects.

Canada in the Global Economy

Historically, Canada's competitive strengths have emanated from its resource endowments—grains, fish and food products, forest products, energy, and basic metals and minerals. However, prospects for rapid export growth in these areas are limited.

In agriculture, Canadian grain producers are more dependent on exports than are American farmers, yet they face the same tough challenges—slow-growing export markets and the adverse effects of agricultural protectionism. In forest products, growth prospects appear constrained by the adequacy of future timber supplies. For many metals and minerals, new technologies and materials have reduced the demand for important Canadian exports (for example, nickel, copper, zinc, and lead), and new sources of supply have reduced many Canadian market shares. In energy, export prices for petroleum and natural gas are currently about half their 1981 levels.

These trends have accentuated a secular decline in the contribution of natural resources to Canadian exports. Forest products, petroleum and natural gas, minerals, and basic metals accounted for 65 percent of Canada's total merchandise exports in 1960, 47 percent in 1970, and about 35 percent in the late 1980s. Much of the decline from 1960 to 1970 was caused by growth in automotive exports, facilitated by the 1965 Automotive Agreement. More recently, the primary causes have been slow-growing global demand for resource products and increasing foreign competition.

As regards secondary manufactures, automotive products' share of Canadian exports has fluctuated significantly, but has averaged about 23 percent over the past two decades. Meanwhile, other manufactures' share increased from 15 percent in 1960 to 19 percent in 1970, to over 25 percent in the late 1980s. This change reflects improved Canadian comparative advantages (or reduced comparative disadvantages) in manufacturing.

In achieving this industrial transformation, Canadian manufacturing firms face many of the same tough challenges confronting their U.S. counterparts, but they are in a weaker position. Canadian manufacturing productivity in 1988 stood at close to 70 percent of U.S. levels, about the same as in 1970. In this regard, underspecialization and slow dissemination of new industrial technologies have historically been key problems. To improve performance, Canadian firms must accelerate rationalization and the implementation of new methods, such as computer-assisted design and manufacturing (CAD/CAM) and flexible manufacturing systems.

Increased competition from U.S. producers will encourage this process; however, it will compound already significant labor adjustment pressures. The results Richardson reviews in chapter 3 indicate that FTA tariff cuts will accentuate the shift in Canadian employment away from the primary sector and toward service activities, leaving manufacturing's overall share of employment virtually unchanged. Within manufacturing, the FTA could induce important interindustry adjustments: textiles, apparel, furniture, and electrical and nonelectrical machinery and equipment, for example, could face losses in employment shares. While most of these FTA-induced adjustments could be accommodated by normal growth and employee turnover, they come on top of other adjustments brought about by global pressures.

Macroeconomic Constraints and Exchange Rates

During the 1980s, U.S. federal budget and current account deficits distorted U.S. patterns of consumption, production, and trade. As the value of the dollar rose about 45 percent[6] from 1980 to 1985, exports, employment, and profits were constrained in agriculture, high-technology manufacturing, and tradeable services; meanwhile, the adjustments that import competition and new technologies posed on resource-based industries and mature manufacturing were intensified. The U.S. current account fell from near balance to a deficit equal to 3.3 percent of the gross domestic product. Manufactures accounted for 85 percent of this drop, accelerating the secular shift in employment to nontradeable services.

For Canada, a strong U.S. dollar was significant, too. From 1979 to 1985, the Canadian dollar fell about 14 percent against the U.S. dollar; it also rose with the U.S. dollar against European currencies and, initially, the yen. However, its appreciation was not as great as that of the U.S. dollar. This improved the competitiveness of Canadian exports in the United States, but weakened it elsewhere. As a consequence, Canada's current account and merchandise trade balances with the United States improved, as they deteriorated and became negative with other countries. The U.S. share of Canadian exports rose from 69 percent to 79 percent.

From 1985 to 1988, the value of the U.S. dollar fell to nearly its 1980 level, and some progress was achieved in curbing federal deficits. Restoring U.S. current account equilibrium will require a reversal of the recent surge in the dollar; a renewed and credible commitment to reducing federal deficits; continued expansion of the Japanese and European economies; and sustained emphasis on domestic demand-led growth, export diversification, and exchange rate adjustments in the East Asian NICs.[7] If these adjustments fail to materialize and large U.S. trade deficits persist, or if macroeconomic policy adjustments result in a severe recession, then protectionist pressures in the United States will mount. This could raise questions about Canada's preferred status in the U.S. market: tighter restraints on steel imports, VRAs or other trade actions in basic nonferrous metals, and more intense competition in industrial incentives could all test the FTA.

Conversely, given an appropriate constellation of U.S., Japanese, European, and East Asian NIC policies, the exchange rate for the dollar that would restore current account equilibrium would likely be lower than that in 1980,[8] and the resulting swing in the U.S. balance on manufactures would impose substantial internal adjustments on U.S. trading partners.[9] These factors could slow growth prospects in the East Asian NICs and require Japan and the EC to reduce domestic savings and increase domestic consumption. The competitiveness of Canadian exports in Europe and Japan would improve at the expense of competitiveness in the United States.[10] Canadian detractors of free trade might then blame an erosion of Canadian competitiveness in U.S. markets on the FTA, even though it would have its basis in macroeconomic adjustments quite independent of the agreement. It is, therefore, important for Canadian policymakers to focus on the consequences of a return to U.S. current account equilibrium and to identify clearly for the Canadian public the sources of regional shifts in Canada's competitive opportunities.

These events also provide the background for the issue of whether the values of the Canadian and U.S. dollars should be linked with the FTA. Two sets of factors are important. First, owing to the dependence of the Canadian economy on U.S. policies and performance, the value of the Canadian dollar already substantially follows the broad movements of the U.S. dollar against other currencies. Canadian banking authorities already face limited trade-offs between the value they seek for their currency and domestically acceptable monetary policies. Second, movements in the Canadian–U.S. dollar rate provide an important safety valve for easing adjustment burdens and avoiding other, protectionist responses as the Canadian economy changes to accommodate free trade.

At this time of considerable instability in the value of the U.S. dollar, some flexibility for the Canadian dollar to trail the U.S. dollar as the latter rises and falls reduces fluctuations in the price competitiveness of Canadian products in Europe and Asia. For the longer term, should productivity rise more rapidly in Canada than in the United States as a result of free trade, some appreciation in the value of the Canadian dollar consistent with current account equilibrium would be likely. Given the complexities created by the combination of instability in the U.S. dollar and the short- and longer-term exchange rate adjustments that may be most consistent with positive structural change in Canada, close consultations between monetary authorities in both countries remain important, but linking the two currencies would not be productive in reducing already limited Canadian policymaking flexibility.

Intra-industry Considerations

Quite apart from interindustry and macroeconomic adjustment issues, structural changes within individual industries have important consequences for the FTA. As U.S. and Canadian manufacturers respond to changing market opportunities, traditional suppliers will not always benefit, because new competitors are winning market shares from long-established firms: for example, consider the growing roles of minimills in steel and Asian firms in North American automobile production. Four factors are important in this regard. First, new computer-based technologies are driving a major retooling of manufacturing and marketing in the most advanced industrialized countries. Second, substantial evidence is emerging that North American manufacturers lag behind Japanese and some Western European competitors in implementing and achieving productivity gains from new industrial technologies.[11] Third, North American firms show enormous variation in their abilities to absorb and profit from new technology. Fourth, large U.S. current account deficits and concerns abroad about American protectionist responses are fueling increased foreign direct investment in North America. These factors set the stage for continued, intense, and counterproductive competitive subsidization among the states and provinces as they seek to attract new businesses and to keep existing employers from moving.

For communities dependent on one or only a few employers, the recovery and expansion of their industries will not necessarily translate into benefits for their labor forces if local employers are not among the more adept North American competitors or if new plants are required to keep, maintain, or reestablish competitiveness. State and provincial governments will encounter continuing political pressures to help finance industrial incentives from communities engaged in bidding wars to attract industry. In turn, pressures will increase on Washington and Ottawa for import relief from communities in danger of losing employers.

Decisions to locate plants in North America usually hinge on considerations other than local incentives. However, as Gary Horlick and Debra Steger point out in chapter 4, neither the states nor the provinces can be expected to stop giving incentives to attract and keep employers unless all the states and provinces do so together. All of this points to the importance of bringing subnational subventions under control and to establishing a binational body to monitor and evaluate adjustment problems, subsidies, and import-relief actions.

Multilateral Negotiations

As U.S. competitive advantages in many agricultural, high-technology, and service industries have narrowed or disappeared, policymakers in the executive branch and Congress, as well as influential leaders in the private sector, have focused increasingly on impediments to foreign market access. U.S. negotiators have worked hard to put agriculture, services, investment, subsidies, government procurement, intellectual property rights, and product standards on the agenda for the Uruguay Round, and to keep these talks moving forward. This agenda includes many of the same issues the United States and Canada are taking up in their FTA negotiations now or at the conclusion of the Uruguay Round, and it is similar to the more ambitious EC 1992 agenda. However, several factors indicate that multilateral progress will be slow.

First, the number and range of development characteristics of participants in the GATT have grown significantly. Coupled with slower growth over the last two decades in North America and Europe, this growth magnifies the adjustment costs that would be imposed on industrial-country producers by further multilateral liberalization. Moreover, many newly industrializing

and developing countries bring different priorities to the negotiating table than developed countries, and views among countries within each of these groups differ in important ways.

Second, progress on nontariff issues, which now dominates
the GATT agenda, often requires harmonization—or at least
greater compatibility—among national policies, practices, and
regulations. This creates problems in several respects. National
practices vary substantially in approaches and rigor even as
countries seek to achieve comparable goals. One example is the
degree to which national governments rely on public ownership,
regulated private firms, or competition to ensure quality and fair
pricing in communications and transportation. Another is national differences in the rigor of technical standards and approval processes for agricultural and food products and
pharmaceuticals. It is more significant, though, that national
governments sometimes differ fundamentally in their basic
goals for public policies. Probably the most striking examples
relate to intellectual property issues, where industrial and several developing countries are separated widely by the importance they assign to the interests of inventors and patent holders,
on the one hand, and benefits of technology transfer and the
interests of consumers, on the other.

Third, the 1992 initiative is taxing the EC's bureaucratic
resources and its capacity for adjustment, perhaps reducing, at
least in the short run, its ability or inclination for participation in
aggressive multilateral liberalization.

By no means do these factors combine to make progress
impossible. However, they do make further meaningful multilateral liberalization more difficult, and they make new regional
agreements and the extension of existing ones more attractive to
policymakers. If the Uruguay Round yields only limited results
on many important issues, then certain questions for the United
States, Canada, and the FTA become more significant: Should
and can the FTA be extended to include Mexico in a North
American free trade area? Should the United States and Canada
seek to negotiate other bilateral agreements? In chapter 5,
Sidney Weintraub examines the potential impact of the FTA on
Mexico and the factors that will likely encourage that country to

seek a process of trade liberalization with its northern neighbors. In chapter 6, I analyze the issues surrounding additional preferential agreements from a U.S. perspective.

Developments in Europe and the FTA

The EC 1992 initiative could have important consequences for Canada's stake in the FTA. To the extent the EC successfully completes its internal market, the twelve member-states will enjoy more open access to a market of about 330 million people than Canada will have to the U.S. market of about 240 million. Canadian firms may find themselves at the same kind of market access disadvantage with respect to nontariff measures that they did a generation ago with respect to tariffs when the EC and FTA were formed. This would provide strong incentives for Canadians to seek harmonization of domestic economic policies and regulations with the United States even more than is currently envisioned under the FTA. Canadians have been concerned that free trade with the United States would force harmonization of domestic economic policies and compromise sovereignty. However, it is important to recognize that pressures for such action do not emanate from Canada's decision to implement the FTA or from U.S. actions. Rather, they spring from broader events in Europe, and the FTA provides Canada with a vehicle for responding to them.

ORIGINS AND CONTENTS OF THE FTA

The idea of a preferential trading relationship between the United States and Canada has a long history. From 1854 to 1866, the two countries engaged in limited duty-free trade.[12] Subsequently, many efforts were made to revive the concept, including the agreement of 1874, which the U.S. Senate rejected; the agreement of 1911, which Canadians rejected in a national election; and the failed negotiations of 1947–1948.[13] During the 1960s and 1970s, the concept again attracted attention among private-sector leaders, academics, and government officials. The endurance of this subject, especially among Canadians, reflects the attraction of secure, free access to the large U.S. market as a means for improving manufacturing productivity and spreading product development costs in high-technology industries. However, Canadians approach commercial relations with the United States cautiously, reflecting profound concerns about the influence of U.S. investment, culture, and politics on their economy and national identity. The decision to seek a free trade agreement with the United States was a bold step for Canada.

Canadian Objectives

Several factors have strongly influenced the evolution of Canadian commercial relations with the United States. Canadian natural resources, being more remote, were generally developed after U.S. resources. Coupled with a much smaller internal market, this encouraged Canadian specialization in resource-based exports. Many of these products are particularly capital-intensive, and this characteristic attracted substantial foreign investment to Canada. Also, Canada's high tariffs encouraged foreign manufacturers to invest in plants there to service the Canadian market. U.S.–Canadian trade has generally reflected underlying comparative advantages; however, trade barriers have reduced specialization, and capital flows have partially substituted for trade flows.

During the 1950s and most of the 1960s, the Canadian economy grew rapidly; Canada was generally open to U.S. investment and had a minimum number of programs for influencing market processes. In the 1970s and early 1980s, policies became more proactive, reflecting Canada's growing concerns about the influence of U.S.–based multinational corporations on its trade patterns, industrial structure, and national life.[14] The Trudeau government adopted industrial policies intended to lessen Canada's dependence on the United States and to improve Canadian competitiveness in nonextractive activities, including aggressive screening of new foreign direct investment through the Foreign Investment Review Agency (FIRA) and the National Energy Program.[15]

The results were mixed. U.S. ownership and control of Canadian industry did decline substantially; however, the U.S. share of Canada's trade did not fall, and these policies failed to improve appreciably Canadian industrial competitiveness.[16] Canada's economic future continues to be linked to U.S. prosperity and policies.

Meanwhile, in the United States, large trade deficits and adjustment problems gave rise to increased protectionist pressures: U.S. trade actions in, for example, the steel and forest products industries and threatened measures in nonferrous metals raised concerns about continued Canadian access to the U.S. market.

Ultimately, Canadians began to seek alternative approaches to economic policy.[17] And a consensus emerged among advocates of a free trade area that Canada's market opportunities in resource products would no longer be sufficient to sustain adequate growth and that Canada therefore must become more competitive in manufacturing. After seven rounds of GATT-sponsored multilateral trade negotiations, Canada's tariffs are no longer sufficient to shield its manufacturing from foreign competition, and foreign tariffs are no longer the major impediment to Canadian exports. The principal obstacles to the restructuring of Canadian manufacturing are foreign nontariff barriers and the threat of new barriers, especially in the United States. U.S. trade actions noted above galvanized the view that U.S. contingent protection was a principal threat to Canadian manufacturing.[18]

Canada's official goals in the bilateral negotiations were fourfold. Canada sought *secure access to the U.S. market* by limiting the effects of U.S. trade remedy laws. It sought exemption from U.S. safeguard actions aimed at third countries and a clearer, bilaterally agreed upon definition of a countervailable subsidy. Also, Canada sought to *enhance access to the U.S. market* by eliminating tariffs and liberalizing nontariff barriers. Among U.S. practices Canadian officials cited were discrimination in U.S. federal and state procurement, product standards, patents, and copyrights. Further, Canada sought to *enshrine these gains* through a strong agreement with an effective dispute settlement mechanism. Finally, it sought to *maintain policy discretion* in cultural industries and foreign investment in some sensitive sectors.[19]

In addition, many in Canada's elite viewed free trade as a way to reduce government intervention in the economy. Canadian negotiators expected to accept constraints on the use of domestic subsidies as part of a bilateral regime for applying countervailing duties, thereby limiting the role of subventions.

U.S. Objectives

For the United States, too, the FTA was an important step. Multilateralism has been the basic thrust of U.S. postwar trade policy. Admittedly, competitive pressures and the limitations of the GATT have caused the United States to manage trade and seek bilateral solutions to trade problems. The United States, for example, entered into a limited free trade agreement with Israel in 1985. However, a comprehensive agreement covering goods, services, and investment with its largest trading partner considerably broadens the scope of U.S. involvement in bilateral arrangements.

U.S. policymakers saw a bilateral agreement with Canada as potentially useful in two ways. First, as discussed above, the attention of U.S. trade policymakers has focused increasingly on the limitations of GATT treatment (or nontreatment) of agriculture, services, and the wide variety of practices that can affect foreign market access for U.S. high-technology products—trade-related investment policies, subsidies, treatment of intellectual property rights, government procurement, and product standards. Many in the U.S. trade policy community saw an agreement with Canada as perhaps providing models for the GATT in several of these areas. Second, they viewed an agreement with Canada as providing a lever in the multilateral process by indicating to the EC, Japan, and others that the United States is prepared to pursue other avenues should the Uruguay Round fail to deliver tangible benefits.[20]

The negotiations offered the United States an opportunity to eliminate higher Canadian tariffs[21] and to enshrine improvements in the trade and investment climate achieved during Prime Minister Pierre Trudeau's final years and under Prime Minister Brian Mulroney. Also, Canada has greatly loosened restrictions on energy exports to the United States, and it again permits some new U.S. investment in that sector. The United States sought assurances that Canada would not again impose aggressive screening and performance requirements on U.S. investment or limit U.S. access to Canadian energy and other resources.

As regards Canadian nontariff barriers, the United States sought to eliminate or reduce discrimination in federal and provincial procurement and impediments to trade created by product and technical standards and testing.[22]

The United States wanted to establish controls on Canadian subsidies and eliminate Canadian duty remissions granted to foreign firms in exchange for sourcing or producing in Canada. In the U.S. view, duty-remission benefits for Asian and European automakers compromised the Automotive Agreement of 1965.

The United States sought a comprehensive agreement on trade in business services and improved market access in financial services.

Essential Elements of the FTA

The FTA makes a good start toward establishing fully integrated markets for goods, services, and capital. It brings down many trade barriers, ensures that most others will not become more restrictive, and establishes processes for reducing still others.[23]

Over the ten-year phase-in period, the FTA will eliminate tariffs,[24] duty drawbacks, and most import restrictions. With regard to automotive products, tariffs in bilateral trade are being phased out on products that meet a tough 50 percent content rule: in contrast to the terms of the old 50 percent content rule the United States applied under the Automotive Agreement, overhead and indirect costs will not count.[25] Canada is phasing out duty-remission benefits for Asian and European automakers that source parts in Canada for export or that have established production facilities there. The FTA prohibits export restrictions (unless grandfathered and except in periods of short supply),[26] export taxes and subsidies, and the dual pricing of exports.

These provisions should ensure most of the benefits of duty-free trade in goods. Americans will enjoy secure access to Canadian energy and other resources at prices comparable to those paid by Canadians. On the downside, the strict 50 percent content rule for automotive products is generally tougher than primary FTA rules of origin for other goods[27] and actually increases the protection afforded parts producers from offshore competition.

Regarding safeguards, during the ten-year phase-in period, tariffs may be restored for up to three years should domestic producers suffer serious injury as a result of bilateral tariff reductions. Each country will exempt the other from GATT article XIX safeguard actions, except in cases where the other is a substantial source of injury; however, in such cases, imports may not be reduced below their trend "over a reasonable base period with allowance for growth" (article 1102, 4.6).

Over the next five to seven years, the two countries have agreed to "develop more effective rules and disciplines concerning the use of government subsidies" and to "develop a substitute system of rules dealing with unfair pricing and subsidization" (article 1907.1). In the interim, the two governments will apply existing national laws; however, judicial review of administrative agency findings will be replaced with binding review by binational panels.

With respect to foreign investment, the United States and Canada will afford each other's subsidiaries national treatment, except in some sensitive sectors. Canada reserves the right to screen only *direct* acquisitions of its largest nonfinancial corporations and financial institutions. Performance requirements directly affecting trade—namely, goals for import substitution and domestic sourcing or exports—are prohibited.[28] Canada's cultural industries are exempt from this and virtually all other provisions of the agreement.

In the area of financial services, U.S. firms will have much greater freedom to expand in Canada. Most barriers to north-south financial integration that will remain emanate from domestic regulations posing impediments to efficient domestic markets—for example, U.S. constraints on interstate banking and the Glass-Steagall Act, which separates U.S. investment and commercial banking. As the two governments continue domestic deregulation, they will seek to assure mutual benefits. The combined effects of the investment and financial services provisions will be to bring a fully integrated U.S.–Canadian capital market much closer.

With regard to *new* practices and regulations affecting business services, the United States and Canada will afford each other's service providers national treatment and the right of establishment, and recognize the need for compatible licensing and certification requirements. This should provide the stable environment necessary for service firms to invest in marketing on both sides of the border—at least within the constraints of existing regulations. The two governments will undertake negotiations to eliminate existing impediments to trade on a sector-by-sector basis.

As for nontariff barriers to trade in goods, the agreement provides a standstill on product standards inhibiting trade and the joint recognition of testing facilities. It lowers the threshold for purchases covered by the GATT procurement code from $171,000 to $25,000—a limited achievement that does not affect the actions of the states and provinces. The FTA prohibits the most significant trade-related foreign investment performance requirements, but leaves unresolved the issue of performance requirements relating to R&D. The agreement does not, however, contain an intellectual property chapter.

The United States and Canada will undertake further bilateral negotiations to harmonize product standards for agricultural products and related commodities; for other goods, they will seek to make product standards more compatible and will recognize each other's testing and certification bodies. The two governments agree to cooperate in the GATT to achieve progress on procurement and intellectual property and to expand the FTA provisions regarding procurement within one year of the conclusion of the Uruguay Round. The Congress would like the issue of R&D- and technology-related investment performance requirements addressed.

The Canada–United States Trade Commission—which consists of the officials of each country who have principal responsibility for international trade, or their designates—will administer the agreement. It will seek to resolve disputes through consensus and will be assisted, where necessary, by binational panels. Binding arbitration may be selected if both parties agree.[29] The agreement does not establish a binational secretariat.

Although the FTA's negotiators achieved a great deal, many of the agreement's benefits are prospective. Among these are the benefits that will be achieved through further discussions on subsidies and dumping, product standards, business and financial services, government procurement, and foreign investment performance requirements.

KEY ISSUES

The FTA is being implemented in a period of rapid change in the international economic system. In the Uruguay Round, negotiators are wrestling with exceedingly complex nontariff issues, making continued multilateral progress difficult, but by no means impossible. The U.S. and Canadian economies are adapting to major changes in the configurations of their competitive opportunities.

The FTA reflects these realities. First, the agreement eliminates tariffs and achieves some immediate progress on nontariff measures; however, as will be the case for multilateral progress, long and elaborate follow-on negotiations will be required to modify and harmonize national policies, practices, and regulations to overcome most remaining impediments to bilateral commerce. For the FTA to achieve its full potential, the United States and Canada will have to devote substantial bureaucratic and political resources to put in force what has already been promised and to bring planned negotiations to meaningful conclusions. Second, although the structural adjustments the FTA is likely to impose would be manageable if taken alone, they come on top of other pressures for change from new foreign competitors and technological advances. All of this raises a panoply of issues regarding the implementation and management of the FTA, prospects for coping with adjustment costs and controlling political pressures for import relief and subsidies, and trade policies toward third countries.

Implementation and Management of the FTA

The FTA did not establish a supranational commission, free-standing secretariat, or binational body to supervise implementation, resolve disputes, undertake investigations, publish records of decisions and investigations, and manage the day-to-day business of keeping a rather complex agreement working smoothly. Instead, a political body composed of two cabinet heads has been put in place to oversee implementation and elaboration of the agreement and to resolve disputes. These officials are supported by quite different bureaucratic structures established within the two governments to conduct the business of the FTA. The U.S. structure is small and dispersed, while the Canadian one is large and more focused. Will U.S. resources prove adequate? Will Canadian bureaucratic emphasis on the FTA distract from meaningful participation in multilateral liberalization? Will these structures be able to cope effectively with the trade policy and legislative prerogatives of the Congress and the autonomy of the provinces?

Should the FTA substantially liberalize bilateral commerce without prejudicing progress in the GATT, the trade policy community will likely judge it a success. Winning the confidence of business, the governments, and the public, especially in Canada, however, will be a more subtle and complex challenge. For example, perceptions about the symmetry of requirements for notification of proposed policies, as well as the constraints ultimately imposed on national actions, will affect Canadian conclusions about equity and fairness.

In chapter 2, David Leyton-Brown describes the institutional structures established within the two governments, contrasting their operational styles and resources. He analyzes the adequacy of these structures and the requirements the FTA must meet to be perceived as a success by business, government, and the public.

Adjustments, Subsidies, and Safeguards

The problems that contemporary adjustment pressures create for the implementation and negotiation of FTA subsidies and safeguard provisions illustrate how difficult it is to manage bilateral liberalization when pressures for structural change, subsidies, and protection are fundamentally global in origin. Given the shifts in competitive opportunities discussed in the first part of this chapter, two kinds of industrial adjustments seem important here. First, in certain situations, market opportunities are shrinking for North American producers, but the industry in one country is in a better position than its counterpart in the other to prosper—for example, Canadian steel and basic nonferrous metals and U.S. household furniture. Second, adequate market opportunities continue for firms based in North America,[30] but a rearrangement of the competitive pecking order among U.S., Canadian, and foreign firms, or the process of established companies' retooling for new technology, sets off intense competition among states, provinces, and communities to attract or keep highly mobile corporate capital and technology, such as automotive plants. In each situation, domestic producers in both countries have displayed strong inclinations to seek subsidies and import relief. Such actions aiding labor and other immobile resources in one country often have a predatory effect on resources in the other.

With more than three-quarters of Canada's exports going to the United States, the effectiveness of the FTA's safeguard provisions to shield it from U.S. import-relief actions, such as programs of VRAs, will be critical to Canada's achieving full benefits under the FTA. In chapter 3, David Richardson examines this issue. He suggests modifications in the FTA's safeguard provisions and a binational committee to help manage import-relief actions.

Bringing subsidies under effective control is a complicated problem for many reasons. For example, although the United States has expressed strong interest in achieving some control over subsidies, an agreement with Canada could result in a discipline covering 100 percent of U.S. subsidies in exchange for a discipline on subsidies in a country accounting for only 20 percent of U.S. foreign trade. Equally significant is the definition of trade-distorting subsidies. When do regional aids count? What about defense and other public procurement preferences? Even more vexing, import relief often has the same bilateral predatory effects as subsidies in distressed industries. All of this illustrates the difficulties of addressing subsidies in a strictly bilateral context or separately from other nontariff issues, such as procurement and safeguards. Nevertheless, FTA article 19 encourages just that.

In chapter 4, Gary Horlick and Debra Steger address the subsidies issue and offer a creative solution. Their proposal includes a committee or structure composed of officials from both governments to review programs. Recognizing that adjustments, subsidies, and safeguards are tightly bound issues, in chapter 7, I suggest that the functions of Richardson's and Horlick and Steger's committees be merged.

Third-Country Relations

The complexities and difficulties of contemporary multilateral negotiations have given rise to interest in regional and bilateral arrangements. Indeed, the FTA has piqued interest in other bilateral and plurilateral arrangements with U.S. trading partners; perhaps the most obvious candidate is Mexico. In chapter 5, Sidney Weintraub examines the impact of the FTA on Mexico, the process of economic reform under way there, and how these give rise to pressures on Mexico to consider a trade agreement with the United States.

The FTA is broadly consistent with U.S. multilateral goals: by strengthening the North American economy, it will improve the U.S. and Canadian ability to participate in future multilateral liberalization. However, it is dangerous to extrapolate that a succession of bilateral or plurilateral agreements would serve the long-term goal of promoting multilateral progress. Other such agreements could create disincentives and institutional barriers to broader progress. By what standards should prospective agreements be judged? In chapter 6, I take up these issues, as well as the FTA's broader implications for U.S. trade policy and the GATT system. Although it is not clear that specific provisions of the FTA provide models for the Uruguay Round, its process does provide important lessons about the modern trade negotiations.

NOTES

1. See Peter Morici, *Reassessing American Competitiveness* (Washington, D.C.: National Planning Association, 1988), pp. 28–54 and 66–81.
2. Since 1969, these have accounted for about 10–15 percent of U.S. current account receipts. In 1988, travel and transportation accounted for the majority, about 9 percent; fees and royalties and private business services contributed only 2 percent and 3 percent, respectively.
3. For example, Japan is already quite competitive in commercial and investment banking, Japan and Korea are in construction and engineering. U.S. firms have lost ground in these industries. See Office of Technology Assessment, *International Competition in Services: Banking, Building, Software, and Know-How* (Washington, D.C.: Government Printing Office, 1987).
4. Exacerbating the effects of these developments for U.S. industry, Japanese manufacturers appear to have overtaken U.S. firms in many advanced materials including metals and alloys, high-performance ceramics, and new semiconductor materials. See Morici, *Reassessing American Competitiveness*, pp. 133–134.
5. Moreover, should the recent surge of the dollar continue, many of the gains achieved by mature industries could be reversed. This would only exacerbate problems in nonferrous metals and steel discussed here.
6. The inflation-adjusted, trade-weighted index of the dollar against forty currencies compiled by the Morgan Guaranty Trust Company.
7. For a discussion of domestic demand-led growth, export diversification, and exchange rate adjustments in the East Asian NICs, see "The Asian NICs: Wrestling with Success," *World Financial Markets*, April 17, 1989, pp. 1–13.
8. The value for the dollar consistent with current account equilibrium has declined because of several factors: (1) U.S. productivity growth has continued to lag behind that of many competitors; (2) more exports are now required to service the external debt; (3) in 1980, the major debtor countries absorbed a quarter of U.S. exports; many of these countries have dramatically cut their current account deficits; (4) U.S. export prospects in agriculture and high technology have been curtailed by the emergence of new suppliers; a lower dollar is the mechanism that would permit compensating improvements in prospects for mature industries; and (5) the sourcing of products from countries with strong currencies—Japan and Germany—can be moved to countries that have more favorable labor costs—Taiwan, Korea, and some members of the Association of Southeast Asian Nations. Also, manufacturers in Germany and Japan can purchase components from these sources to maintain price competitiveness in the U.S. market.

9. See Morici, *Reassessing American Competitiveness,* pp. 117–118.

10. Other things being equal, the U.S. share of Canadian exports would be expected to decline (probably to the levels of the late 1970s or early 1980s), but effects of FTA tariff cuts should moderate this trend.

11. For more detailed discussion of these issues, see Richard Cyert and David C. Mowery, eds., *Technology and Employment: Innovation and Growth in the U.S. Economy* (Washington, D.C.: National Academy Press, 1987), pp. 122–128; Morici, *Reassessing American Competitiveness,* pp. 40–46 and 120–133; and Ramchandran Jaikumar, "Postindustrial Manufacturing," *Harvard Business Review* 64, no. 6 (November/December 1986), pp. 69–76.

12. The Reciprocal Free Trade Agreement, a part of the Elgin-Marcy Treaty of 1854, established duty-free trade between the United States and the British North American Territories of Canada (present-day Ontario and Quebec), New Brunswick, Newfoundland, Nova Scotia, and Prince Edward Island. The agreement covered agricultural and forest products; ores and metals; dairy products; animal, fish, and kindred products; and only a few manufactures (dyestuff and rags). From 1855 to 1863, about 55 percent of U.S. exports entered Canada duty-free, while about 90 percent of Canada's exports entered the United States duty-free. For more detailed accounts of this agreement and the period from 1854 to the mid-1980s, see Anna Guthrie, "A Brief History of Canadian-American Reciprocity," in Sperry Lea, ed., *A Canada–U.S. Free Trade Arrangement: Survey of Possible Characteristics* (Washington, D.C., and Montreal: Canadian-American Committee, 1963), appendix A; J. L. Garanstein, "Free Trade between Canada and the United States: The Issue that Will Not Go Away," in Dennis Stairs and Gilbert R. Winham, eds., *The Politics of Canada's Economic Relationship with the United States* (Toronto: University of Toronto Press for the Royal Commission on Economic Development Prospects for Canada, 1985); and Peter Morici, "U.S.–Canada Trade Relations," in Peter Karl Kresl, ed., *Seen from the South* (Provo, Utah: Brigham Young University Press, 1989).

13. After World War II, Canada encountered serious balance-of-payments difficulties; one solution considered was a bilateral trade agreement that would encourage economic development along lines more complementary to that of the United States. In 1948, a free trade agreement emerged as the likely outcome of secret negotiations; however, Prime Minister Mackenzie King developed second thoughts about establishing such close ties with the United States.

14. Many Canadians perceived increased economic integration with the United States as fostering cultural and social integration. For example, in discussing expanded commercial ties, a 1970 Canadian white paper on foreign policy stated: "While such developments should be beneficial for Canada's growth, the constant danger that sovereignty, independence and cultural identity may be impaired will require a conscious effort on Canada's part to keep the whole situation under control." See Department of External Affairs, *Foreign Policy for Canadians* (Ottawa, 1970), p. 24.

15. Other tools of this industrial policy were extensive financial incentives to promote increased natural-resource processing, secondary manufacturing, regional development, and technology-intensive activities; aggressive

federal and provincial purchasing policies; efforts to steer private procurement in major resource projects to Canadian suppliers; and duty-remission programs to encourage foreign manufacturers to source components or locate plants in Canada.

16. In 1988, for instance, Canadian manufacturing productivity stood at about 70 percent of U.S. levels, the same relative level as in 1970.

17. For example, the federal government undertook an important investigation of alternatives—the Royal Commission on the Economic Union and Development Prospects for Canada (the Macdonald Royal Commission)—which, in 1985, recommended free trade with the United States.

18. See Minister for External Trade and Secretary of State for External Affairs, *Canadian Trade Negotiations* (Ottawa: Department of External Affairs, 1985). That document states, "the threat of countervail has proven to be a major deterrent to investment in Canada" (p. 26).

19. Ibid., pp. 3–4 and 25–27.

20. In 1988, then Treasury Secretary James Baker stated: "This agreement is also a lever to achieve more open trade. Other nations are forced to recognize that the United States will devise ways to expand trade—with or without them. If they choose not to open markets, they will not reap the benefits." See "James Baker: The Geopolitical Economy of U.S.–Canada Trade Pact," *International Economy* 1, no. 2 (January/February 1988), pp. 34–41.

21. At the conclusion of the Tokyo Round tariff cuts in 1987, average Canadian tariffs on U.S. imports were 9–10 percent; the comparable figures for the United States were 4–5 percent. See Clayton Yeutter, "Testimony before the Senate Committee on U.S.–Canada Trade Negotiations," April 11, 1986, p. 3.

22. The United States also sought to end discrimination against the marketing of U.S. liquor, wine, and beer; barriers to U.S. exports of poultry, eggs, dairy products, and red meats; and seasonal tariffs on fresh fruits and vegetables. The FTA addresses U.S. concerns about liquor, wine, red meats, and fresh fruits and vegetables, but not about beer, poultry, eggs, and dairy products.

   In addition, the United States sought to resolve a number of other bilateral issues, including better protection for U.S. pharmaceutical patents and copyright protection for U.S. broadcasters whose signals are retransmitted in Canada. The FTA addresses these concerns.

23. This section is not intended to be a complete summary of the FTA. Readers requiring one should see Peter Morici, "The Canada–U.S. Free Trade Agreement," *International Trade Journal* III, no. 4 (Summer 1989); and _____, "The Canada–U.S. Free Trade Agreement: Origins, Contents and Prospects," in Thomas Hyclak and Robert Thornton, eds., *Economic Aspects of Regional Trading Agreements* (Brighton, Eng.: Wheatsheaf, 1989).

24. Rules of origin require materials and components imported from third countries to be incorporated into other goods or transformed in physically or commercially significant ways. In most cases, this is achieved if a production process results in a change in tariff classification or, as a backup requirement, if it results in a 50 percent U.S./Canadian value added. However, the tougher 50 percent rule is required for automotive products,

and the FTA limits the amount of apparel made from offshore fabric that qualifies for duty-free treatment.

25. Under the Automotive Agreement of 1965, Canada essentially affords duty-free treatment to all the imports of firms that assemble one car in Canada for each car sold there and achieve value added in Canada equal to 60 percent of their sales there. The United States affords duty-free treatment to the Canadian-made products of firms meeting a 50 percent U.S./Canadian content requirement. The incentives for Chrysler, General Motors, and Ford to meet the Canadian safeguards are duty-free access for U.S.–produced cars and duty-free access for offshore imports. Among the major foreign makers of passenger vehicles, only Volvo qualifies for these benefits.

   By meeting the old Canadian content rules, the three major North American companies and Volvo may continue to bring captive imports into Canada duty-free. In the FTA, Canada agrees not to extend such benefits to other foreign passenger vehicle manufacturers.

26. During periods of shortage, the two countries must share available supplies on the basis of consumption patterns for the previous three years. Also, subject to GATT disciplines, both countries may restrict exports of logs, and Quebec and the Atlantic provinces may restrict exports of unprocessed fish.

27. See note 24.

28. Canadian officials maintain that other performance requirements—such as undertakings concerning product mandates, R&D spending, and technology transfers—are now accepted and legitimized, because the FTA does not prohibit them. U.S. officials do not share this view. See chapter 2, pp. 49–50, and chapter 6, pp. 135–136.

29. Disputes regarding safeguards are subject to binding arbitration.

30. These include subsidiaries of overseas corporations.

2

IMPLEMENTING THE AGREEMENT

David Leyton-Brown

Negotiating the Canada–U.S. Free Trade Agreement (FTA) was only the beginning of the story. Implementation of the FTA will be an ongoing process for years to come. That process will touch on economic, social, and political sensitivities in both countries. For the United States, the FTA is a trade agreement, albeit one that deals also with a number of related economic issues. Canadians see the FTA as much more than a trade agreement—it marks a new relationship with the United States, and it therefore has a bearing on all bilateral issues, whether economic or not. Consequently, the success of the FTA will be measured not only by objective economic criteria, but also by more subjective political consequences, as the process of implementation unfolds.

The legislation that was necessary to bring the FTA into force on January 1, 1989, has been enacted in each country, and most of the necessary regulations are in place. The required institutional mechanisms, internal and bilateral, have been established, or are in the process of being created and altered. However, they are just beginning to operate, and only time will tell how effectively they will be able to perform the functions intended for them, and to respond to the foreseeable and unforeseeable challenges that will confront the United States and Canada in the FTA. The course of future negotiations, dispute settlement, compliance with specific provisions of the agreement that might have politically sensitive consequences, and response to developments and challenges from the economic environment will determine the success with which the FTA is implemented, and the confidence with which it is received by governments, the business communities, and the public in both countries.

This chapter will examine the implementing legislation in each of the two countries, with regard to the legislative processes by which it was produced and to differences in content. Second, it will contrast the style of operation and magnitude of bureaucratic resources committed to internal institutional structures within each government. Third, it will assess the nature and adequacy of the bilateral institutional mechanisms and notification and consultation procedures established under the FTA, especially with respect to their ability to deal with Congress, provincial governments, and the world beyond North America. Fourth, it will identify the differing governmental, business, and public priorities and perspectives out of which confidence in the successful implementation of the FTA will be expressed, and the likely challenges facing the FTA that will test that confidence. Finally, it will consider some implications for future trade policy of the two countries.

IMPLEMENTING LEGISLATION

In both the United States and Canada, implementing legislation had to be passed to bring the FTA into force. The legislative processes involved were not identical, and observers in each country may benefit from some background clarification of how the legislation emerged in the other.

The United States

The FTA was negotiated under the accelerated implementing authority, or fast-track, provision of the U.S. Trade Act. Under this provision, once submitted to Congress, the implementing legislation had to be passed or voted down, without any possibility of amendment, within ninety legislative days. As of January 2, 1988, when the FTA was formally signed, ninety legislative days did not remain in the 1988 congressional session, because of the timetable for presidential nominating conventions and the elections. This fact, coupled with perceptions of a protectionist Congress, led some Canadians to fear that the legislation might not be passed before the expiration of the fast-track authority at the end of 1988.

However, a clear understanding emerged between the administration and Congress, expressed in an exchange of letters on February 17, 1988, that if the administration agreed not to submit the FTA implementing legislation until June 1, Congress would guarantee legislative action before the end of that congressional session. The administration committed itself to working with Congress in drafting the implementing legislation (subject to conformity with the principles of the FTA). Indeed, it had consulted closely with appropriate committees of Congress throughout the negotiating process and during the period from October 3 to mid-December 1987, when the elements of the agreement were being translated into the formal language of the FTA.

In the normal legislative process, after legislation is introduced, it proceeds to markup, subcommittee, committee, House of Representatives and Senate, and conference before final enactment into law. Under the fast-track process, a great deal of congressional work anticipates and replaces these stages before the legislation is formally introduced. From February through May 1988, the relevant subcommittees and committees held public hearings, "nonmarkup markup" sessions, committee approval of draft legislation, and a "nonconference conference" to reconcile differences between the drafts worked out separately by each body with the administration.

Since the legislation had not yet been formally introduced, the relevant committees could not consider the language of that legislation in a markup session. However, they did the functional equivalent on unofficial texts in "nonmarkup markup" sessions before the legislation was introduced. Similarly, since the House of Representatives and Senate had not yet passed different versions of the legislation, there could not be a conference to reconcile the two versions; but representatives of the two houses, in a "nonconference conference," reconciled their different versions of the draft legislation before it was even introduced, let alone passed. These activities performed the functions of markup and conference, but at different stages of the legislative process, thus allowing Congress to participate in shaping the draft legislation without violating its commitment not to amend the legislation once introduced.

Both the House and the Senate informally approved the resulting package of draft legislation in July; only then, on July 25, did the president formally introduce the legislation. It received speedy passage in both bodies, by a vote of 366–40 in the House on August 9, and 83–9 in the Senate on September 19.[1]

Such rapid passage represented neither conspiratorial glee nor indifference to the agreement. The amount of congressional time and attention devoted to the agreement during the free trade negotiations, and especially during the drafting of the implementing legislation, was more than commensurate with its importance to both countries. Despite the many special interest groups whose problems the FTA did not solve, and who opposed particular provisions of the FTA or wished to see additional ones, the vote in both the House and the Senate was overwhelmingly one-sided. Senators and congressmen who had the opportunity to pander to constituency pressures without threatening the passage of the legislation resisted that temptation. Whether the margin of the vote is explained by satisfaction with the agreement, a sense of inevitability of the process, inherent goodwill toward Canada, or the fact that all the deals that could be done were done in the negotiating and drafting process, very few senators and congressmen actually voted against the legislation.

Canada

Canada has no equivalent to the fast-track process. The implementing legislation was treated no differently than any other piece of legislation. It required three readings in both the House of Commons and the Senate, and royal assent, before being proclaimed. It could be amended, and in fact was (though only on technical aspects, and in ways acceptable to the government).

The House of Commons, with its substantial Progressive Conservative majority, passed the implementing legislation by the end of August 1988. However, the Liberal majority in the Senate unexpectedly delayed passage of the legislation to force a parliamentary election, and the implementing legislation died on the order paper.

The election campaign focused primarily on the FTA. Supporters emphasized its success in insulating Canada from U.S. protectionism and giving Canada a voice in future negotiations, its opportunity for rationalization and increased international competitiveness, and its secure and enhanced access to the U.S. market for exports and the U.S. economy for investments. Opponents made three arguments. Some argued that they favored free trade, but the FTA was a bad deal, in which Canada would give up too much and receive too little in return. Others were simply opposed to this or any other free trade agreement, preferring instead some combination of managed trade and industrial policy. A third group saw the FTA as a threat to Canadian autonomy and independence. They characterized it as giving the United States a voice in, or veto over, future Canadian policy, thus endangering Canadian social and regional development programs; as imposing pressures for increased harmonization of policies, thus making Canada more and more like the United States; and as leading to the erosion of Canada's cultural identity.

The Mulroney government won reelection in November, with a majority of seats in the House of Commons, but without a majority of the popular vote. The country was deeply divided over the free trade issue, and an unsettled public environment remains.

Parliament was rapidly recalled after the election, and new implementing legislation was introduced. The Liberal majority in the Senate, which was unchanged by the election, could have continued to oppose the legislation, or at least could have resorted to unexceptionable parliamentary procedure to delay passage and embarrass the government. They did neither, but accepted the election result as a mandate for the FTA. The implementing legislation was passed through all of the necessary stages in time to bring the agreement into force as scheduled, on January 1, 1989.

Differences in the Legislation

The legislative process aside, certain technical differences distinguish the U.S. and Canadian implementing legislation. The U.S. legislation establishes a thirty-month fast-track period for any subsequent legislation that may be necessary to make U.S. law compatible with the FTA. That said, U.S. law will prevail over the agreement in the event of any inconsistencies, because the burden is on the U.S. government to make any necessary statutory changes, rather than leaving the FTA to override problems in the future (that is, it is incumbent on the administration and Congress to identify every U.S. law that must be changed to bring it into compliance). The FTA does prevail over any inconsistent state law, and the federal government can and must challenge any such inconsistencies.

The U.S. legislation, and the accompanying Statement of Administrative Action, specified objectives for the U.S. government in future negotiations with Canada. In so doing, it defined priorities (at least on the part of Congress) for the future unfolding of the FTA. These priorities are, of course, not binding upon the other party to that agreement, but they are indicative of issues that will be pressed.

The Canadian implementing legislation created new legislation where none existed before (for example, spending authority, procedures should a province decide not to abide by the obligations regarding wines and spirits,[2] and the creation of a procurement review board) and amended existing legislation to achieve consistency.

The Canadian legislation does not amend every act that could potentially be in conflict with the FTA (though it does explicitly amend over two dozen pieces of legislation). Where the governor-general-in-council (that is, the cabinet) has discretionary power in issuing regulations, the legislation assumes that the cabinet will take the FTA into account. The Canadian legislation does not anticipate any future legislation that might emerge from the FTA process, leaving it to be handled through the regular legislative process, as was the implementing legislation itself. It does not impose a regulatory scheme on the provinces, and it contains no blanket override clause, because Parliament cannot legislate in areas of provincial competence and so could not override provincial laws in such areas. The implementing legislation deals entirely with areas of federal competence, where no provincial override is necessary.

In both countries, legislative involvement will continue not only through possible subsequent legislation, but also through required legislative monitoring of the FTA's implementation. In the United States, a legislative oversight committee of Congress has been charged with that function, while in Canada, the Senate Committee on Foreign Affairs has been assigned that role.

INTERNAL INSTITUTIONAL STRUCTURES

The differences between the United States and Canada are not simply those of legislative process. There are also differences of philosophy and operating style, which resulted in the creation of varying institutional mechanisms to implement the FTA. The free trade negotiations were conducted on the U.S. side by a small negotiating team drawing on a variety of interdepartmental and interagency networks, and on the Canadian side by a large, dedicated trade negotiator's office. This difference carries over into the resulting institutional structure within each country. The consequence is reminiscent of the findings of the literature on complex interdependence between the two countries: The allocation of bureaucratic resources to bilateral issues tends to be asymmetrical. More, and more senior, senior personnel in Canada than in the United States are devoted to Canada–U.S. relations; this difference can serve to offset the asymmetry of power.[3]

The United States

Institutional activity within the U.S. government regarding the FTA will be small and dispersed; as implementation proceeds, this could result in problems of bureaucratic rivalry.

The key figure, and the chief U.S. representative on the Trade Commission, will be the U.S. trade representative. Within that office a small core unit will center on a whole series of interdepartmental and interagency groups, which will maintain a liaison and formulate policy. The dedicated resources might be quite small, but impressive depth can be brought to bear with great speed. The permanent secretariat called for in chapter 19 of the FTA will be located within the Department of Commerce. This secretariat will be responsible for administrative matters related to the operation of the binational dispute settlement panels and committees, but will not have a policy function. The fundamental U.S. economic policymaking mechanism will probably continue to be the Economic Policy Committee, chaired by the secretary of the treasury. The State Department, with its concern for the management of the Canada–U.S. relationship, will inevitably be involved, especially because Secretary James Baker played an important individual role in the final negotiations of the FTA and will be personally as well as institutionally committed to its success.

Canada

A large bureaucratic structure dedicated solely to the policy and management issues related to the FTA has been established as a branch within the Department of External Affairs (DEA); it reports in parallel with the U.S. branch, to a senior assistant deputy minister. In bureaucratic terms, the departmental rival has swallowed the previously independent Trade Negotiations Office, eliminating many problems of coordination by absorbing the other major actor.

This new branch will be structured as two bureaus (responsible for trade policy and for management), each with three divisions, along with general legal counsel. The trade policy divisions will deal with trade policy vis-à-vis the United States, tariffs and market access, and trade relations (that is, day-to-day trade irritants, like section 301 cases, shakes and shingles, softwood lumber, and so on). The management divisions will be responsible for federal-provincial relations and a private-sector liaison, free trade coordination (to ensure that other government departments do what is required with regard to FTA commitments), and the permanent secretariat called for under chapter 19.

Despite its size and complexity, this branch will not be the sole repository of interest or expertise concerning the FTA in the Canadian government. For example, a departmental task force within Revenue Canada will deal with tariffs, and another in the Department of Employment and Immigration will handle relevant FTA questions. The branch is not structured to represent all interested departments, but will link with the other departmental groups through an interdepartmental committee structure. A jurisdictional struggle is under way for control over some aspects of FTA implementation. The contenders are International Trade Minister John Crosbie, who is the minister designated in article 1802.2 of the FTA as the government's principal representative, and whose predecessor oversaw the free trade negotiations, and Finance Minister Michael Wilson, who is responsible for tariff policy and federal spending, and who was personally involved in the final days of negotiation of the FTA when the ultimate compromises were reached. Both sought responsibility for naming the roster of candidates for the dispute settlement panels, and both wish to sit on the Trade Commission.

The mode of operation and interaction of these new institutional structures within each government, and the new institutional mechanisms between the two governments, will largely determine the impact of the FTA on the conduct, style, and substance of Canada–U.S. relations. In particular, the relationship between the respective foreign ministers, who are the principal cabinet officers responsible for Canada–U.S. relations, and the newly created bilateral institutional mechanisms, in which neither is represented, could spell either effective coordination or operation at cross-purposes. The objective is for government policy in each country to be formulated and implemented coherently, with full recognition of contexts and relative priorities across the range of bilateral issues. It is possible, though, that different cabinet officers, departments, and agencies could operate inconsistently, each pursuing its own agenda and indifferent to, or even in conflict with, other government policies. The possible connections among trade, environmental, defense, and other issues on the Canada–U.S. agenda will test the ability of both governments internally and jointly to manage this complex relationship.

BILATERAL INSTITUTIONAL MECHANISMS

The principal institutional mechanism between the two countries is to be the Canada–United States Trade Commission, established under chapter 18 of the FTA. Interestingly, neither the 1854 trade reciprocity arrangements nor the 1911 attempt to establish a free trade area proposed specific machinery to administer the relationship.[4] The commission is charged to supervise the implementation of the FTA, to resolve disputes that may arise over its interpretation and application (except in cases regarding financial services or antidumping and countervailing duties), to oversee its future elaboration, and to consider any other matter that may affect its operation.

In trying to understand what sort of mechanism the commission will be, it is perhaps best to be explicit about what it is not. During the free trade negotiations, public attention focused on two models, at opposite ends of the spectrum, but each was rejected. On the one hand, the commission is not a supranational body, such as the Commission of the European Communities, with a permanent staff of international civil servants and with supranational decision-making powers. On the other hand, it is not an advisory body modeled after the International Joint Commission, to serve mainly as a fact-finding mechanism on matters referred to it by the two governments, and offering them recommendations rather than making decisions.[5] Instead, it is a political body, composed of political leaders rather than functionaries, intended to make decisions, but lacking any dedicated secretariat or single repository of records, precedents, and experience.

The impact of the commission on the conduct, style, and substance of Canada–U.S. relations is hard to predict in advance of final decisions about its composition and experience of its practice. It is, however, possible to raise some questions that might sensitize observers to important issues in its evolution.

The first question concerns the adequacy and effect of the notification function. The FTA stipulates that "each Party shall provide written notice to the other Party of any proposed or actual measure that it considers might materially affect the operation of the Agreement" (1803.1). Stephen Clarkson, one Canadian analyst, has suggested that this notification obligation would require an unprecedented reporting capability, far beyond what the existing DEA or Department of State could manage, which would involve continuing reports from all departments, Crown corporations, and related agencies. He foresees that in both countries, but especially in Canada, the commission's notification function will lead to the expansion of government regulation and to increased centralization of the federal system.[6]

Of even greater consequence is whether the requirements for notification and consultation will have an equal impact on both Canada and the United States. There is some reason to expect that the sorts of measures to which the notification and consultation provisions refer are more predictable and manageable in the Canadian parliamentary system than in the U.S. congressional system. If the perception or the reality emerges that the FTA constrains the Canadian government more than the U.S. government in the development of national policies—because of the ability of Congress to introduce unexpected amendments or compromises at late stages in the legislative process—the commission, and the entire FTA, will be suspect in Canada. On the other hand, if monitoring forthcoming provincial measures, and therefore realizing the notification and consultation provisions in that regard, proves difficult, U.S. dissatisfaction may grow.

Related to this question is one concerning the ability of the commission to deal with the "wild cards" in each country's political system—that is, Congress in the United States and provincial governments in Canada. Congress has historically resisted any infringement on its autonomy and is likely to be an elusive or reluctant party to the commission's actions. Where the commission's dispute settlement procedures result in a decision for nonimplementation or removal of a measure not conforming to the FTA (1807.8), and where the measure in question is embodied in congressional legislation, how effective will the commission be in overriding that legislation, and how compliant will Congress be in accepting the primacy of the commission in restricting its freedom of action? Ideally, of course, the notification procedures should head off such legislation before it is enacted, but if that does not occur, perhaps because of the notification problems discussed above, the question of nonimplementation or removal of some piece of congressional legislation could become painfully relevant.

Similar questions arise in Canada about the commission's ability to bind or reverse provincial government policies. This may be politically relevant because two of the ten provincial premiers have not given their support to the FTA.[7] The question of provincial compliance has understandably been of concern to U.S. negotiators and legislators from the beginning of the free trade negotiations, and it remains unanswered in the context of the expected ongoing operation of the commission.

The compliance of Congress and the provinces with the commission's decisions assumes that such decisions can be reached. Questions remain about the workability of the decision-making process of the commission. The commission is designed to make all decisions by consensus (1802.5), which is surely easier to reach in a bilateral relationship than in a multilateral one involving dozens of other parties. Nevertheless, one may wonder whether even a two-party consensus can be reached in what may appear to be a zero-sum competitive situation, or one in which the facts as well as the interests are in dispute. The issue would be quite different in the event of a dispute over action flagrantly violating the FTA (for example, by Congress or a provincial government) or a dispute arising out of established practice.

The findings of the expert panels to which the commission may refer a dispute should be an important element in defusing political tension over disputes. The FTA prescribes that if initial consultations within the commission do not result in agreement on a settlement of the dispute in question, the matter shall be referred to a panel for arbitration (in cases of emergency actions, or when both parties agree) or, for a report containing findings of fact, determination of whether the matter is inconsistent with the obligations of the agreement, and recommendations for resolution of the dispute. The nonpolitical and, one hopes, objective activity of such panels is an integral part of the operation of the institutional mechanism.

The FTA does provide for the inability of the commission to reach agreement on a mutually satisfactory resolution within a specified time, by authorizing the complainant to suspend the application of benefits of equivalent effect to the other party until the parties have reached agreement on a resolution to the dispute (1807.9). That provision could, however, simply add another dispute on top of the existing one, if the two sides disagree about the "equivalent effect" of the retaliatory measures. This is likely to be the case, unless a panel has identified to the satisfaction of both parties the magnitude of the effect of the measure in question.

The commission is the institutional centerpiece of the FTA, but it is not the only mandated institutional mechanism. The agreement calls for two rosters of panelists for dispute settlement panels—those under chapter 18 for general dispute settlement and arbitration, and those under chapter 19 for binding review of final antidumping and countervailing duty decisions. Furthermore, the FTA calls for many working groups to study or conduct negotiations on such matters as unfair pricing and government subsidization, the state of the North American automotive industry, and agricultural standards.

BUILDING CONFIDENCE IN THE FTA

The FTA is a living agreement, designed to evolve and adapt through the operation and interaction of these mechanisms. Its successful implementation will rest not only on the immediate effects of tariff cuts and other market opening measures, but also on the degree of confidence in its process. To gauge that confidence as it unfolds, it is necessary first to recognize whose confidence is involved. In each country, government, business, and public perspectives may respond to different priorities and reach different assessments.

Government Perspectives

Each government will view the FTA in internal, bilateral, and external contexts. On the internal level, the FTA may alter interdepartmental rivalry or coordination for the better or for the worse. It will be welcomed if it provides a context and structure for the organization of policy, but not if it becomes yet another issue over which individuals, departments, and agencies compete for budget, influence, and prestige. The agreement may also improve or complicate relations between governmental branches (in the United States) or levels (in Canada). It may be enjoyed as an occasion for legislative-executive harmony of interest and approach, or resented as another source of strain between the president and Congress. In Canada, it could offer economic benefits long sought by many provincial premiers or, in disputes over notification and compliance, could become a source of federal-provincial jurisdictional conflict. It may constrain policymaking (through provisions such as those concerning energy or investment) or help to resolve outstanding policy issues.

On the bilateral level, the U.S. and Canadian governments will judge the FTA according to whether it improves or worsens the overall management of the two countries' relationship. It may result in the resolution of irritants between the two countries, or at least in their depoliticization, or it may trigger new problems. The dispute settlement mechanisms promise to do the former, but the FTA itself will create new issues over which conflicts may arise. The FTA may affect the climate and process of managing noncommercial issues. It has focused attention on the bilateral relationship in both countries, but may thereby also have increased sensitivity to explicit trade-offs. Will reaching an agreement on acid rain reduction be easier or more difficult with the FTA in place?

Finally, both governments will be concerned about the impact of the FTA on relations with third countries. If the agreement makes dealing with others easier or more effective—for example, through cooperation in negotiations at the Uruguay Round—officials of both governments will receive it as a boon. On the other hand, if it creates or compounds conflicts with other countries, its value will be questioned.

Business Perspectives

The business communities in both countries will judge the FTA to be a success if it results in increased bilateral economic activity, making the world's largest bilateral economic relationship even larger. Canadian business will react positively if the economic effect of tariff removal, let alone increased and more secure access to the U.S. market, enhances the international competitiveness of Canadian industry. In general, business in both countries will welcome increased export and investment opportunities, but oppose increased import competition.

In the United States and especially in Canada, the business communities strongly supported the FTA, but some differences of interest and priority can be expected to appear as the agreement is implemented. The FTA does not satisfy all industries equally: it fulfills the particular objectives of some, but defers those of others for later attention. In particular, some U.S. firms in the nonferrous metals industry and other natural resource and energy sectors probably will seek to restrain alleged Canadian domestic subsidization. U.S. financial services firms can be expected to seek to expand market access for financial services. Some firms in both countries opposed the agreement from the outset, and others will be harmed by it or will fail to take advantage of the opportunities created. Particular responses to adjustment problems will vary widely.

Business in both countries has been heavily involved in the FTA process through governmental advisory groups, and through active political support. Especially in Canada, the initiative for opening the free trade negotiations was largely business-driven. The business community will continue to be the driving force behind many future developments, such as negotiations for acceleration of tariff reductions. In each country, business organizations will be reorganized, and resources allocated, to monitor the unfolding implementation of the FTA. Liaison between the business community and government on FTA issues will occur in Canada through the reorganized International Trade Advisory Committee and sectoral advisory groups, and in the United States through the Advisory Committee on Trade Negotiations, four policy advisory committees (agriculture, defense, industry, and science), and ad hoc technical groups. The business criteria for success of the FTA, however, are not necessarily the same as those of governments. Ending or avoiding a dispute to the satisfaction of governments may not produce a result that is economically optimal for one or all of the private interests involved.

Public Perspectives

The question of public confidence in the FTA will be most prominent in Canada. Relations with the United States dominate Canada's economic and political agenda, while the U.S. agenda is more diversified. Despite the Mulroney victory in a Canadian election fought mainly on the issue of the FTA, the debate in Canada is not over. The next election will probably be fought on the issue of whether the FTA has been beneficial or detrimental for Canada; until then, attacks on and justifications of the FTA will dominate Canadian politics. While the U.S. public is far from indifferent to the results of the FTA, the importance of the agreement's being viewed as a success is greater in Canada. Until the Canadian public sees and accepts a positive payoff from the FTA, the debate will continue.

Canadian critics and proponents of the FTA will focus in part on the question of harmonization between the two countries—not only the technical and narrow question of harmonization of standards agreed to in the FTA, but the broader issue of harmonization of social and economic policies. Of course, harmonization pressures already emanate from the business communities, from U.S. policy, and from the international trade and monetary system. One of the principal concerns of Canadian critics of the FTA, and one of the principal themes of the recent Canadian election campaign, is whether the agreement will accelerate these trends. The ability of the FTA's institutional mechanisms to deal with the appearance and the reality of harmonization will be of great significance in allaying Canadians' concerns. This is a matter not just of symbolism and public relations, but of sensitivity to the political context in which its development will be received. Commitments in the agreement must be honored, but no impressions must emerge of further harmonization as inevitable or coerced. The Canadian government must communicate to its citizens that it deliberately sought and entered into any future harmonization in Canada's interest, while the U.S. government must be careful not to appear to force the issue, just as it was in the initiation of the free trade negotiations themselves.

FUTURE CHALLENGES

Inevitably, as the FTA is implemented, more U.S.–Canada conflicts and tensions will arise than have before, which will test the confidence of these different groups. This will be so because of the persistence of traditional and predictable irritants, along with the emergence of new issues generated by and through the FTA. The latter will include ongoing negotiations, conflicts to be handled through the dispute settlement mechanisms, different expectations or interpretations about provisions of the agreement, and changes in the economic environment.

Negotiations

The FTA does not resolve all economic and commercial issues between the United States and Canada. In many areas, the FTA explicitly aims at future expansion. Successful implementation of the FTA rests in part on the ability of the two governments to bring to a successful conclusion the rich agenda of ongoing negotiations mandated by the agreement, which includes the following:

- Develop a substitute system of rules and disciplines for anti-dumping and countervailing duties, to deal with unfair pricing and government subsidization (1906 and 1907).[8]

- Improve and expand the government procurement provisions of the FTA, not later than one year after the completion of the Uruguay Round negotiations (1307).

- Accelerate tariff reductions on specific items (401.5).

- Extend coverage of the FTA to additional service sectors (1405).

- Assess the state of the North American automotive industry and measures to improve its competitiveness (1004).

- Make compatible standards-related measures and product approval procedures, accreditation, and acceptance of test data (608).

- Further facilitate the temporary entry of businesspersons (1503.b).

- Cooperate in the Uruguay Round and elsewhere to improve protection of intellectual property (2004).

- Review outstanding issues related to retransmission rights, after the implementation of FTA provisions (2006).

- Establish working groups to make equivalent and harmonize technical regulations and standards in the agricultural sector (708).

- Work together for multilateral elimination of agricultural subsidies in the Uruguay Round and elsewhere (701).

- Consult at least semiannually on agricultural issues (709).

- Consult regularly on the effective administration or revision of the rules-of-origin provisions (303).

- Consult with respect to proposed changes in customs administration (406).

- Consult to facilitate and increase tourism, and eliminate impediments to trade in tourism services (annex 1404, B,4).

- Consult regarding financial services (1704).

Of all of these negotiations, the most important is the one regarding new rules for dealing with unfair pricing and government subsidization (1907). Some observers consider these five-to-seven-year negotiations as valuable regardless of outcome, mandating a degree of close consultation not possible without the FTA.[9] Nevertheless, these negotiations are likely to be the animus for the entire FTA implementation and, at least in Canadian public perception, to be the benchmark for success of the new trade relationship.

The extent to which the negotiations result in a substantive agreement on new rules, that do not impair Canadian social programs and health care, and that further insulate Canada from unilateral U.S. trade remedies, will be important in determining how receptive the Canadian public is to the negotiations and to the future of the FTA. The extent to which the negotiations result in a substantive agreement on new rules that impose more discipline on the subsidy behavior of Canadian governments and do not impair the ability of the U.S. government to operate its trade remedy system will be important in shaping the receptivity of the U.S. public to the same immediate- and longer-term issues. These are not mutually exclusive outcomes, and the negotiations are not a zero-sum game.[10] A compromise could identify the following: which programs are permissible and which are prohibited, which direct payments are prohibited and therefore subject to retaliatory action only above an agreed percentage of capital costs or operating expenses, and which alleged indirect subsidies remain subject to a revised countervailing duty procedure. This could provide more discipline while sheltering social programs, and protect legitimate U.S. business interests while maintaining Canadian latitude for certain regional development programs. It is, however, the case that satisfaction with the process and outcome of these negotiations will be determined as much subjectively as objectively, and will be affected by the way in which issues and agreements are presented to the business communities and the public in both countries.

Dispute Settlement

The FTA created several dispute settlement mechanisms. These are a process of binding binational review for antidumping and countervailing duty cases; compulsory arbitration for safeguard cases; panels of experts to offer recommendations in cases referred to them; and a high-level political body, the Canada–United States Trade Commission, to supervise the implementation of the agreement and resolve disputes over its interpretation. Successful implementation of the FTA will rest on the demonstration that these dispute settlement mechanisms work in the variety of disputes that can be expected to come before them.

In the initial testing period, it will be very important for Canadians to see that the dispute settlement mechanisms work effectively, because of their sensitivities to the asymmetries of size and power between the two countries. Especially in the area of antidumping and countervailing duties, working effectively may be equated with overturning or restraining a U.S. decision. However, for Americans to see them as working effectively, the dispute settlement mechanisms must not appear to be one-sided or to impair reasonable protection from Canadian subsidies. Again, this need not lead to zero-sum thinking, so long as citizens of both countries perceive fairness and predictability in the mechanisms' operation.

The early cases handled through the dispute settlement mechanisms will go a long way toward shaping public perceptions of their effectiveness. In the first two cases, which Canada launched within seventy-two hours after the FTA came into force, both governments were scrupulous about complying with the provisions and timetables of the agreement, trying to make the dispute settlement mechanisms work as designed.[11]

The types of disputes with which these mechanisms will have to deal can be predicted in general, if not in specific. Cases involving antidumping and countervailing duties, safeguards, or the general dispute settlement mechanisms will arise when special interests seek relief from alleged injury or harmonization pressure, or when the public or government in either country perceives a denial of expected benefits or a constraint against adopting new policies.

In a democratic society, private interests beset by external competition or adjustment pressures predictably seek political intervention on their behalf. That can take the form of resorting to established trade remedies, or of direct legislative action. In an uncertain international economic environment, and in the context of adjustment pressures resulting from the FTA, the initiatives from the private sector in both countries for protection of their interests can be expected to increase, as the benefits and costs of the agreement are distributed unevenly. The beneficiaries of the FTA are not always those in greatest need.

$150 million, by 1992. However, even the higher threshold will not allow acquisition of approximately 100 of the largest Canadian-owned companies without review. Furthermore, cultural industries are exempt from this provision and therefore still subject to review, and existing measures restricting access in other sectors—such as energy, transportation, and financial institutions—are grandfathered. Reviewed investments could still be permitted to proceed, but some prospective U.S. investors could be frustrated to find that the door to investment in Canada is not as wide open as they had hoped and expected.

Finally, the two governments have agreed not to subject investors from each other's country to trade-related performance requirements—namely, those demanding commitments for import substitution, domestic content, or export levels. Here, however, lies an important difference of interpretation. Canadian officials readily concede that they have a commitment not to impose trade-related performance requirements, but they argue that because non-trade-related performance requirements (those concerning research and development or job training, for instance) are not forbidden, they are legitimized and accepted, at least tacitly. Some U.S. officials differ with this interpretation, arguing that this sort of performance requirement should not be considered accepted, simply because it was left to be taken up later. They see a difference between what is grandfathered, what is accepted, and what is not mentioned at all. This difference of expectations could possibly be the root of future tension if one government acts upon an understanding not shared by the other.

Another possible source of tension in the investment area could be the national treatment provision prohibiting the future imposition of U.S. review of Canadian investment. If congressional sensitivity toward foreign direct investment in the United States continues to mount, and legislation establishing some form of investment screening results, the FTA requires that Canada be excluded from such measures. This may be surprising and unwelcome to private interests and legislators pushing for restrictions on foreign investment in the United States.

Energy relations between Canada and the United States have also been the focus of tension.[13] Against the backdrop of that stormy past, it is perhaps surprising that both governments view the FTA's energy provisions so positively. Simon Reisman, Canada's chief negotiator in the free trade negotiations, has publicly stated that the energy chapter of the FTA is one of two in which he takes the greatest pride.[14] Clayton Yeutter, the U.S. trade representative at the time of the negotiations, has called the energy chapter the jewel of the agreement. This happy unanimity is not because of identical interests, but because each is pleased with a different part of the chapter.

Canada gained an assurance of secure access to the U.S. market for its energy exports, which has been a long-standing Canadian objective. The United States gained proportionate access to Canadian supplies in times of supply shortages, and an assurance of nondiscriminatory pricing of Canadian energy exports (that is, an end to the two-price system, which provided lower prices for Canadian consumers). Depending on supply and price developments in the international energy market, one or the other of these benefits will be more salient, and one or the other of the countries may consider its benefits eroded. In a future period of abundant energy supplies, Canada will benefit from secure access to the U.S. market, but will be alarmed if political pressures arise in the United States on the part of electricity, uranium, or natural gas interests to restrict or limit that access. In the event of energy shortages, the United States will benefit from the guarantee of access to the same proportion of total Canadian supply it imported in the previous thirty-six months, but that is bound to be a source of tension if Canada's energy needs go unmet, and especially if Canadians perceive (rightly or wrongly) that U.S. imports were inflated in the preceding period in anticipation of the coming shortages.

Canadian cultural policy has also been a traditional source of contention with the United States.[15] Canada has sometimes sought to pursue its cultural policy objectives with measures that have a discriminatory impact on U.S. interests. An example was its effort to ensure a financially viable private television broadcasting industry to convey Canadian cultural content to Canadian viewers: in July 1971, it required that Canadian cable television companies "simulcast," and authorized them to phase in "commercial deletion";[16] and in 1976, it amended the Income Tax Act to deny tax deductibility for the costs of advertising directed primarily to a Canadian market but broadcast by a foreign (that is, U.S.) station. The purpose, and effect, of these measures was to divert advertising revenue from U.S. border broadcasting stations to Canadian stations, thus contributing to the financial viability and continued existence of the latter. The United States has tended to treat resulting problems purely as trade disputes, without acknowledging Canada's genuine cultural concerns and objectives that gave rise to the policies in question. The FTA has dealt with this conundrum in a fashion that elicits divergent responses.

One article of the agreement (2005.1) exempts cultural industries from the provisions of the FTA, seemingly allowing the Canadian government to pursue cultural policy unfettered by the agreement. The next article (2005.2), however, the so-called retaliation clause, authorizes either party to "take measures of equivalent commercial effect in response to actions that would have been inconsistent with this agreement but for paragraph 1."

Critics of the FTA charge that this takes away with one hand what was apparently given with the other. Canadian cultural nationalists charge that this clause gives the United States control over future Canadian cultural policy, by threatening retaliation (in unrelated areas) against, and therefore cabinet opposition to, any cultural policy initiative.[17] Proponents of the FTA, however, argue that this clause puts a ceiling on allowable U.S. retaliation, thereby forever preventing another escalatory incident like the border broadcasting dispute. In that case, Congress retaliated against the changes in the Canadian Income Tax Act mentioned above, which diverted $15–$20 million per year in advertising revenue from U.S. border broadcasting stations to Canadian stations, by refusing to exempt Canada from U.S. legislation denying tax deductibility for expenses of attending conventions in foreign countries. This convention tax measure cost the Canadian economy an estimated $100 million per year,[18] more than five times what the Canadian policy cost the U.S. border broadcasters.

Given the political sensitivity in Canada to the effects of the FTA on Canadian culture and cultural policies, it is inevitable that the retaliatory clause will be put to the test. This is an issue that will affect governmental, business, and public perceptions of the success of the FTA.

Economic Environment

Changes in the economic environment—within the United States and Canada, and in the world more broadly—will seriously affect successful implementation of the FTA. If the Bush administration proves unable to reduce significantly the trade and budget deficits now hampering the competitiveness of the U.S. economy, the provisions and process of the agreement could come under attack. If current economic expansion gives way before the twin deficits are substantially reduced, a rise in protectionist pressures in the United States—especially in Congress—seems inevitable, and the currently benign environment for the FTA could evaporate.

The international environment could also change, presenting additional problems for the FTA. Exchange rate volatility, which is not unrelated to the condition of the U.S. trade and budget deficits, can pose further challenges to the international competitiveness of U.S. and Canadian firms, quite apart from their underlying comparative advantage. An international economic downturn would have major implications for U.S. and Canadian export opportunities abroad, and for the desire of foreign firms to export to North American markets. Energy relations between Canada and the United States are heavily dependent on price and supply developments in the international energy industry. To a considerable extent, the FTA's successful implementation will depend upon the response of the United States and Canada, and of the institutional mechanisms and processes of the agreement, to external developments beyond the control of either or both of the governments.

Canada and the United States also face very real challenges in their evolving economic relations with the rest of the world. As the European Community moves toward the establishment of a single internal market in 1992, as Japan moves toward uncertain but closer economic relations with countries of the Pacific Rim, and as various developing countries pose competitive threats to both Canada and the United States in some of the politically most sensitive sectors, important questions emerge about how well the institutional mechanisms of the FTA will be able to relate outward as well as inward. In the short run, the United States and Canada must persuade their other trading partners that the FTA complies with the General Agreement on Tariffs and Trade (GATT), and must follow through on the explicit commitments to cooperate in the Uruguay Round negotiations. In the longer run, the United States and Canada must be able to identify their common interests vis-à-vis other trade groupings, and act jointly to advance them, especially if the Uruguay Round fails to make satisfactory progress on all of the key matters on its agenda.

Bilateral trade disputes between Canada and the United States often have their origins in differing national responses to common problems in the changing international environment.[19] Preoccupation with visible and proximate competitors rather than with joint and distant challenges can lead to politically satisfying, bilaterally disruptive, and economically unproductive solutions. The current international competitive pressures on the steel and automobile industries of both the United States and Canada are only prominent examples among many such cases.

The FTA creates not a customs union (with a common external tariff) but a free trade area, with some of the policy harmonization features of an economic community. Many Canadians are vigilant in their opposition to any greater degree of economic integration, because of their fear that it will lead to ultimate political unification. Nonetheless, joint problems require joint solutions. One of the ongoing challenges for the FTA institutional mechanisms will be to respond jointly to external challenges, without offending domestic sensibilities in the process. To do so requires sensitivity in political presentation, being careful not to take the other party for granted (or appear to do so), to claim excessive credit before one's domestic audience for the results of common actions, or to seek to compel the other country's compliance with a unilateral position.

IMPLICATIONS FOR POLICY

The United States and Canada will both face important policy questions apart from the implementation of the FTA provisions themselves. Some of these will be joint matters, especially as regards the way the FTA relates to outside countries. The need to demonstrate that the FTA complies with the GATT and the need to deal with "cherry pickers," who want to avail themselves of particular features of the overall agreement, are examples. Should the results of the Uruguay Round be disappointing, the FTA could be the vehicle for forging joint initiatives. Other questions will be particular policy concerns for one government or the other.

The United States

Peter Morici addresses the ramifications of the FTA for the future of U.S. trade policy in chapter 6, where he concentrates especially on lessons to be learned from the FTA experience, on what the agreement reveals about the core U.S. agenda, and on implications for relations with third countries. Sidney Weintraub also addresses this last question, with regard to the most likely candidate for some sort of additional trade arrangement with the United States—that is, Mexico.

The issue of trade relations with third countries concerns not only the question of whether the FTA can be extended to include others, or matched by one or more other bilateral agreements. The larger question concerns the apparent attractiveness of regional trading groups, and whether or not the FTA portends a trend in which the United States will turn away from the multilateralism of the GATT and lean toward bilateralism.[20] One objective of the United States in entering the free trade negotiations with Canada was clearly multilateral—that is, to provide impetus to the multilateral negotiations of the Uruguay Round. The United States, having realized that objective, is bound to retain a vested interest in further liberalization of trade with the rest of the world, rather than to turn inward in North America, because of the structure of its trade. While almost 80 percent of Canadian trade is covered by the FTA, almost 80 percent of U.S. trade is with countries other than its FTA partner. No matter how important trade is between the United States and its largest single trading partner, the major U.S. trade policy instrument is bound to remain the GATT, which manages trade between the United States and its many large trading partners.

The greatest policy challenge for the United States with regard to the FTA itself will be to give priority to its implementation at a time when many other large concerns demand attention from the same individuals and institutions—for example, combating the trade and budget deficits, the international struggle over agricultural subsidies, the scheduled end of the Uruguay Round in 1991, and the onset of the single market in Europe in 1992. Many highly placed individuals in the U.S. government have personal interests in the agreement's implementation, but there will also be competing priorities. The tendency might be to regard the FTA as a "done deal," and turn attention elsewhere, to the detriment of the success of FTA processes.

Canada

Canada will resist dilution of the economic gains it anticipates from access to the U.S. market, but will not seek to perpetuate a preferential trading system. In terms of bilateral and plurilateral relations with third countries, this means that Canada will be unlikely to favor extension of the FTA to other participants, especially if that reduces Canadian competitiveness in the U.S. market and erodes the trade-offs made in the agreement, without seeking compensating advantages to be realized through that process.

The bigger policy question for Canada will be whether implementation of the FTA will cause Canada to deemphasize the GATT and the multilateral trading system. Will Canada have put all, or at least most, of its eggs in the bilateral basket?

The Canadian public stance is sure to be strong, continued support for the GATT. It will be important for the Canadian government to show its trading partners, and its own citizens, that its eggs are not entirely in the U.S. basket. Beyond that political expediency, it is also economically important for Canada to continue to recognize the importance of the GATT. The FTA did not deal with all Canada–U.S. trade issues (for example, it left unresolved questions regarding agriculture and intellectual property), and did not go as far as hoped on all matters. Furthermore, an expectation of Canadian trade policy is that the FTA will increase the international competitiveness of Canadian industry, which will in turn increase Canadian penetration of markets other than that of the United States. Indeed, because Canada's traditional highest objective in multilateral trade negotiations of a deal with the United States has already been achieved, Canada will be free in the Uruguay Round and elsewhere to devote its energies to other priorities, such as enhanced trade relations with other trading partners or strengthening the international trading system. As a consequence, Canada could be, and be perceived as, an active and major player in the multilateral negotiations.

However, it will be important to distinguish between the political appearance of a public stance and negotiating activity, and the reality of allocated resources. Despite the high quality of the personnel assigned to work on the multilateral trade negotiations, the vast majority of the Canadian trade bureaucracy will be committed in the next few years to the implementation of the FTA. That effort will be mirrored by the attention and organization of the majority of the Canadian business community. The FTA matters proportionately more to Canada than it does to the United States, and it will devote resources accordingly.

THE SUCCESS OF THE FTA?

Because of the FTA, the future within and between the United States and Canada will be different from the past. Commitments have been made, institutions and procedures have been created, and problems will be faced. The way in which the implementation process unfolds, and responds to the challenges confronting it, will affect the atmosphere in which the FTA evolves, and the confidence that governments, business, and publics have in the agreement. That confidence will determine how successful, and how far-reaching, this agreement will be for the overall relationship between the two countries.

In objective economic terms, the FTA will be judged a success if it results in increased economic activity between the two countries, and increased competitiveness of industry in the United States and, especially, Canada. In subjective political terms, the criteria are harder to define explicitly; they depend upon the interpretation of the governmental, business, or public observer.

The dispute settlement mechanisms must be seen to work effectively, and thus must demonstrate fairness and predictability of treatment, even-handed rather than one-sided outcomes, compliance with the disciplines imposed by the FTA, and restraint of unilateral action outside the agreement's mechanisms and procedures. The ongoing and future negotiations mandated by the FTA must lead to visibly successful outcomes. In particular, the subsidies negotiations to develop new rules dealing with unfair pricing and government subsidization must succeed in resolving an issue that was too difficult to be concluded in the original free trade negotiations, and that remains the focus of great concern in both countries. The FTA must enhance—and not impair—the effectiveness of the United States and Canada in responding to developments and challenges in the external environment. Finally, it must make it easier—and not harder—to manage the complex and interdependent relationship between the two countries. The extent to which all of these criteria are met will be the political test of the implementation of the agreement.

NOTES

1. The Senators who voted against the legislation were Jeff Bingaman (D.-N. Mex.), Quentin Burdick (D.-N. Dak.), William Cohen (R.-Maine), Kent Conrad (D.-N. Dak.), Pete Domenici (R.-N. Mex.), Wendell Ford (D.-Ky.), Carl Levin (D.-Mich.), John Melcher (D.-Mont.), and George Mitchell (D.-Maine).
2. Article 9 authorizes the issuing of regulations binding on any province to give effect to chapter 8 of the FTA dealing with wines and spirits, which would not come into force with respect to any province that is in confor-

mity with the provisions of that chapter. This apparently cumbersome provision simply means that the federal government will act to enforce this obligation of the agreement only if a province does not comply.

3. Robert O. Keohane and Joseph S. Nye, *Power and Interdependence* (Boston: Little, Brown & Co., 1977).
4. Maxwell Cohen, "Canada and the US—New Approaches to Undeadly Quarrels," *International Perspectives* (March/April 1985), pp. 17–18.
5. Frank Stone, "Institutional Provisions and Form of the Proposed Canada–United States Trade Agreement," Discussion Paper in International Economics, no. 8604 (Ottawa: Institute for Research on Public Policy, 1986).
6. Stephen Clarkson, "The Canada–United States Trade Commission: The Political Implications of CUSTER for Canada," in Marc Gold and David Leyton-Brown, eds., *Trade-offs on Free Trade: The Canada–U.S. Free Trade Agreement* (Toronto: Carswell, 1988), pp. 160–167.
7. These are David Peterson of Ontario and Joe Ghiz of Prince Edward Island.
8. See chapter 4 of this volume.
9. Richard G. Lipsey, "The Free Trade Agreement in Context," in Gold and Leyton-Brown, *Trade-offs*, pp. 67–78.
10. Horlick and Steger propose a new set of rules for subsidization and countervailing remedies that could be in the interest of both countries. See chapter 4.
11. One case involves the U.S. definition of wool; the other, the intended retention of tariffs on Canadian plywood because of a dispute over eligibility of certain grades of U.S. plywood for residential construction in Canada.
12. Gary Clyde Hufbauer and Andrew James Samet, "Investment Relations between Canada and the United States," in Willis C. Armstrong, Louise S. Armstrong, and Francis O. Wilcox, eds., *Canada and the United States: Dependence and Divergence* (Lanham, Md.: University Press of America for the Atlantic Council of the United States, 1986), pp. 103–151; and David Leyton-Brown, *Weathering the Storm: Canadian–U.S. Relations, 1980–83* (Toronto and Washington, D.C.: Canadian-American Committee, 1985), pp. 23–42.
13. Leyton-Brown, *Weathering the Storm*, pp. 43–56; and Edward F. Wonder, "U.S.–Canada Energy Relations," in Armstrong et al., *Canada and the United States*, pp. 65–101.
14. The other is the automotive goods chapter.
15. Leyton-Brown, *Weathering the Storm*, pp. 57–70.
16. Ibid., p. 59. "Simulcasting" means that when a Canadian and a U.S. station on the same cable system are simultaneously broadcasting the same program (though not, of course, the same advertising), the cable television company is to feed the Canadian signal on both channels. "Commercial deletion" means that a cable television company may remove and replace the commercials contained in the broadcast signals of a station not licensed to serve Canada.
17. See, for example, Rick Salutin, "Culture and the Deal: Another Broken Promise," in Gold and Leyton-Brown, *Trade-offs*, pp. 365–369.

18. Leyton-Brown, *Weathering the Storm*, pp. 60–65.
19. David Leyton-Brown and John Gerard Ruggie, "The North American Political Economy in the Global Context: An Analytical Framework," *International Journal* XLII, no. 1 (1986/1987).
20. William Diebold, Jr., ed., *Bilateralism, Multilateralism and Canada in U.S. Trade Policy* (Cambridge, Mass.: Ballinger for the Council on Foreign Relations, 1988).

3

ADJUSTMENTS AND SAFEGUARDS

J. David Richardson

As discussed in chapter 1, the Free Trade Agreement (FTA) is being implemented coincident with major changes in the configurations of U.S. and Canadian competitive opportunities in global markets. Coupled with rapid technological advances in both products and manufacturing processes, these changes are confronting firms, workers, and public policymakers with substantial adjustment challenges. FTA-induced industrial rationalization will further complicate these challenges even as the agreement creates new growth opportunities. This chapter examines Canadian and American adjustment capabilities and the pressures the FTA is likely to impose that would test these capabilities.

Two types of adjustment capability are relevant. One is the array of generalized policies facilitating the movement of labor and business resources from one activity to another.[1] The second is the safeguard provisions that are the contingent flexibility of every trade agreement. Without flexibility to recontract on a sector-by-sector basis in the face of unforeseeable adjustment pressures, most trade agreements would be unappealingly risky and rigid, and would never materialize.[2]

Adjustment pressures have two sources in the FTA. First, the agreement will provoke economic restructuring across the bilateral border in response to the removal of various barriers. Second, it will moderate or aggravate the provocations to each economy from underlying changes in the rest of the world.

This essay sizes up how important these sources of adjustment pressure are to Canada and to the United States. Next, it considers whether general adjustment capability and the agreement's very GATT-like safeguard provisions are up to the task of coping with these adjustment pressures. Its general tone is questioning, in the face of growing cross-border mobility of "corporate capital." Such capital is highly sensitive to the sectoral and regional subsidies that were a dominant issue in the negotiations. Adjustments, safeguards, and subsidies are thus inextricably linked. Finally, this chapter explores the linkage further, and suggests how Canada and the United States might reconsider safeguard provisions as they negotiate disciplines for subsidies. Specific reformulations of FTA safeguard provisions might include targeting of workers, small firms, communities, and immobile resource owners only, not large firms; and the gradual development of an arms-length agency, representing the collective interests of both countries, and responsible for disseminating information, monitoring adherence to the FTA, and publicizing relevant progress and pressures. Discussion of and experimentation with such reforms might prove quite useful for ongoing multilateral negotiations on safeguards.

ADJUSTMENT PRESSURES FROM THE CANADA–U.S. FREE TRADE AGREEMENT

A large number of careful studies are available of the bilateral adjustments forced on workers, firms, and industries by free trade between Canada and the United States. Rather than surveying them all here, the discussion below singles out several of the most recent, and draws some conclusions.[3]

By comparison, a smaller number of studies are available about how the FTA alters Canadian and U.S. adjustment to global pressures.[4] An attempt is made below to summarize their conclusions.

Bilateral Adjustment Pressures

Table 1 summarizes one recent study of the long-run effects of bilateral trade liberalization between Canada and the United States. The study, by Drusilla Brown and Robert Stern, is noteworthy for permitting estimates of bilateral adjustment pressures on both workers and firms (or perhaps plants) in Canada and the United States.[5] Its chief weakness is that its estimates are for tariff abolition across all sectors, not accounting for the

TABLE 1. LONG-RUN EFFECTS OF TARIFF ABOLITION ON ALL TRADE
BETWEEN CANADA AND THE UNITED STATES
(projected percentage change)

Sector	ISIC Group[a]	Market Structure[b]	Entry[c]	Employment Canada	Employment U.S.	Number of Firms Canada	Number of Firms U.S.
AGRICULTURE, FORESTRY, FISHING	1	PC	F	−5.6	−0.5	—	—
MINING AND QUARRYING	2	MS	N	−1.1	−0.5	0.0	0.0
MANUFACTURING	3			−0.2	−0.4		
Food, beverages, tobacco	310	MC	F	−1.9	0.0	−2.7	0.0
Textiles	321	MC	N	−35.4	3.9	0.0	0.0
Clothing	322	MC	F	−6.4	0.7	−8.6	0.7
Leather products	323	PC	F	4.9	−0.6	—	—
Footwear	324	MC	F	2.2	−0.5	−1.4	−0.6
Wood products	331	PC	F	−6.1	0.5	—	—
Furniture and fixtures	332	MC	F	−2.5	0.8	−13.6	−0.8
Paper products	341	MC	F	−19.3	3.1	−19.1	1.9
Printing and publishing	342	MC	F	−3.3	0.2	−3.1	0.0
Chemicals	35A	MC	N	17.9	0.8	0.0	0.0
Petroleum products	35B	MS	N	−11.6	0.2	0.0	0.0
Rubber products	355	MS	N	−1.2	0.1	0.0	0.0
Nonmetallic mineral products[d]	36A	MC	F	−16.8	0.9	−17.2	0.9
Glass products	362	MS	N	−3.9	0.4	0.0	0.0
Iron and steel	371	MS	F	28.5	−0.5	7.2	−0.5
Nonferrous metals	372	MC	F	152.4	−13.6	150.3	−13.6
Metal products	381	MC	F	−7.1	0.7	−9.0	0.7
Nonelectrical machinery	382	MC	N	−1.2	−0.3	0.0	0.0
Electrical machinery	383	MC	F	−14.2	1.2	−18.1	−0.4
Transport equipment	384	MC	N	0.5	0.0	0.0	0.0
Miscellaneous manufactures[e]	38A	MC	F	7.3	−0.5	−13.2	0.1

TABLE 1 *continued*

Sector	ISIC Group[a]	Market Structure[b]	Entry[c]	Employment Canada	Employment U.S.	Number of Firms Canada	Number of Firms U.S.
SERVICES				0.5	0.0		
Utilities[f]	4	MS	N	0.1	−0.3	0.0	0.0
Construction	5	PC	F	1.0	0.0	—	—
Wholesale trade[g]	6	MC	F	0.5	−0.1	0.3	0.0
Transportation[h]	7	MC	F	0.5	0.0	0.3	0.1
Financial services[i]	8	MC	N	0.4	−0.1	0.0	0.0
Personal services	9	PC	F	0.5	0.0	—	—
AGGREGATE				0.0	0.0		

Sources: Drusilla K. Brown and Robert M. Stern, "Computable General Equilibrium Estimates of the Gains from U.S.–Canadian Trade Liberalization," Presented to the Conference on Economic Aspects of Regional Trading Arrangements, Lehigh University, Bethlehem, Pennsylvania, May 25–27, 1988, University of Michigan Research Seminar in International Economics Discussion Paper, no. 220, Tables 3, 7, 8; and Alan V. Deardorff and Robert M. Stern, *The Michigan Model of World Production and Trade* (Cambridge, Mass.: MIT Press, 1986), pp. 37–38, 70–71, 74–75.

[a]International Standard Industrial Classification.

[b]PC = Perfectly competitive markets (firms earn normal profits and have minimal markups of price above marginal cost). These are assumed in nationally differentiated goods.
MC = Monopolistically competitive global markets. These are assumed in goods that are differentiated across firms (whose market power is reflected in the size of their markups of price above marginal cost).
MS = Markets are separated from each other by national border barriers, such as transport costs, and homogeneous goods are produced in each by imperfectly competitive firms (whose market power is reflected in the size of their markups of price above marginal cost).

[c]F = Free entry of new competitors and free exit of incumbent firms is assumed.
N = No entry is assumed; existing firms remain active.

[d]Including pottery, china, and earthenware.

[e]Plastic products not elsewhere classified, professional photographic goods, and other manufacturing industries.

[f]Electricity, gas, and water.

[g]Including restaurants and hotels.

[h]Including storage and communications.

[i]Including insurance and real estate.

— Indicates that the change in the number of firms under perfect competition is not generally considered very significant because of their large number, small size, and low barriers to (ease of) entry and exit.

grandfathering, exceptions, and liberalization of nontariff barriers that are in fact part of the agreement.[6] Brown and Stern also allow an estimate of whether interindustry adjustment pressures are large, or whether adjustment pressures are of the more innocuous intra-industry variety.[7] Their findings may be viewed as an upper bound on interindustry pressures by comparison with the results of other studies.[8] The value of an upper bound is to answer the question, How bad might the pressures get?

The principal conclusion from Table 1 is that Canadian workers may indeed face moderate interindustry adjustment pressures. This summary conclusion springs from several components.

First, estimated structural adjustment appears much larger in Canada than in the United States. This is to be expected in proportional terms; in total number of positions and firms (plants) gained or lost across all sectors, U.S. adjustment pressures are almost as large.[9] U.S. adjustment pressures are, however, much less convincingly injurious, as the term is usually defined for purposes of trade policy relief.

Second, adjustment pressures on firms appear comparable to those on workers. The estimated sectoral effects of the FTA on numbers of firms and workers are of similar sign and size. Appearances are deceptive, however. Adjustment pressures on firms are more moderate than they appear, to the extent that firms are diversified across *sectors,* especially those with estimates of opposite signs; firms are diversified across the *border* between the last two columns of the table, especially those with estimates of opposite signs; or firms are diversified across *time,* having foreseen more integrated continental markets even before the agreement was sealed, and having gradually "preemptively adjusted."[10]

Third, adjustment pressures on Canadian workers to move across sectors, and not just within them, may be significant, even accounting for a ten-year phase-in. Five of the twenty-one manufacturing sectors are estimated to experience double-digit declines in employment from what would otherwise have been the case—that is more than 1 percent per year over the phase-in period. These sectors are textiles, paper products, petroleum products, nonmetallic mineral products (including pottery, china, and earthenware), and electrical machinery. Clothing, wood products, and metal products experience declines of more than 0.5 percent per year. On the other hand, declines of up to 1 percent per year may be easily absorbed by normal turnover—quits, hires, and so forth—even for trade-sensitive industries, as the Economic Council of Canada has documented extensively.[11]

Fourth, Canadian manufacturing employment overall shrinks by a minuscule 0.2 percent, but labor and other resources become much more specialized on a mix of miscellaneous and basic manufactures (chemicals, iron and steel, and nonferrous metals, with a very small increase in transport equipment). U.S. manufacturing employment rises by 0.4 percent, spread widely across sectors, with significant decline only in nonferrous metals. Correspondingly, total manufacturing jobs in the integrated North American economy rise slightly less than 0.4 percent, easing the overall continental adjustment pressures on manufacturing.

Finally, employment in agriculture and mining is estimated to fall in both countries as rationalization of manufacturing and services draws resources away. In Canada, such resources are estimated to flow predominantly toward services, with manufacturing almost holding its own; in the United States, toward manufacturing, with services almost holding its own.[12]

Brown and Stern's estimates represent worst-case limits, since most other research finds smaller, less frequently negative employment effects at this level of aggregation. The studies by Sunder Magun and Someshwar Rao and by Richard Harris and Victoria Kwakwa are two recent and noteworthy examples finding more moderate effects.[13] Each includes positive forces counteracting those featured in the Brown and Stern study. One force is the estimated 2–4 percent gain in Canadian labor productivity implied by the rationalization that many studies predict. This tends to boost long-run wages in all sectors, and the number of workers who must move experience smaller earnings losses than otherwise, compared with their historical norm.[14] A second positive force is the buoyancy that rationalization may impart to forecasts of Canadian investment prospects, making growth trends temporarily more positive and recessions less likely. Furthermore, Harris and Kwakwa show how empirically realistic steady growth in output and employment in the Canadian economy can virtually erase all transitional adjustment pressures of the Free Trade Agreement on labor; normal turnover of workers is more than enough to absorb the margin of workers displaced by the agreement.[15] Harris and Kwakwa also estimate that wages in general will rise quickly above their historical trend, even during the phase-in period.

In sum, calculations of bilateral adjustment from the FTA show potential for some pressure on Canadian workers to shift jobs across sectors. Such pressure is moderate, however, not catastrophic, even in the worst-case calculations. Thus, predicted recourse to adjustment mechanisms ranges from little to moderate.

Global Adjustment Pressures

No study has detailed the incremental adjustment pressures from global competition that the FTA might invite or allay. In chapter 1, Peter Morici discusses the general issue and provides background documentation. Three examples of such incremental pressures that may be quantitatively significant, especially for Canada, spring from European integration, from Mexico's unique situation, and from U.S. macroeconomic realignment.

The FTA may significantly reduce Canadian adjustment pressures from Europe's 1992 initiative. By integrating economically with the United States, Canada may share the U.S. capacity to resist any closure of export markets through "Fortress Europe" tendencies, and by having rationalized before Europe, Canada may find it easier to meet stronger European competitiveness in its own and third-country markets.

On the other hand, by integrating with the United States, Canada may have increased its exposure to adjustment pressures from Mexican competition, rules of origin notwithstanding. To the extent that trade diversion from Mexico is a result of Canada–U.S. arrangements, as Sidney Weintraub suggests in chapter 5, two things may happen. First, Mexico may seek some sort of limited accession that would force both Canada and the

United States to confront new adjustment pressures. Second, even in the absence of a Mexican policy initiative, formal and informal resource movement from Mexico to the United States may increase, so that "Mexican" resources (with U.S. residence!) may find it easier to penetrate Canadian markets than they did before the FTA was signed.

Finally, to the extent that the Canadian economy is now better integrated with the U.S. economy than it was before the agreement, its exposure to macroeconomic adjustment pressure caused by U.S. needs to trim its trade deficit may have increased.[16]

ADJUSTMENT CAPABILITY AND SAFEGUARD PROVISIONS OF THE AGREEMENT

Canada and the United States have strengthened adjustment policies and established new safeguard provisions. But how effective will these steps be in view of the increased mobility of corporate capital?

Generalized Adjustment Policies

Both Canada and the United States have general policies that facilitate the movement of resources from one activity to another. Workers are helped to adjust through unemployment insurance, advance notification, vesting, severance requirements, job-search assistance, government-supported training and retraining programs, and (in Canada) mobility allowances.[17] For firms, adjustment is an important goal of government-sponsored support for small business, research and development, and export activities, and of laws covering bankruptcy, antitrust, merger and acquisition, and fair pricing.[18]

Most commentators think that these general policies are reasonably effective during normal fluctuations. But both Canada and the United States have recently considered changes to strengthen them, especially in positive-adjustment relative to safety-net dimensions, and especially for workers and communities. In Canada, the Advisory Committee to the Government on Adjustment has recently issued its recommendations, and in the United States, Congress has recently passed a new annual $1 billion dislocated worker program with a state-based allocation of funds that varies with long-term unemployment.[19]

Furthermore, each country recognizes that trade-related adjustment pressures are often especially severe or politically sensitive. As a result, each has a supplementary system of sectoral safeguards to ease and facilitate adjustment to international competition.[20]

Safeguards

Safeguard provisions of the FTA are widely thought to break new ground, as are the provisions for dealing with unfair trade and countervailing duties. While it is clear that the latter provisions are indeed innovative, it is not so clear that those pertaining to safeguards are.

The agreement's procedures in chapter 11 are basically the same as article XIX of the GATT, suitably modified to recognize the compatibility of the bilateral agreement with GATT article XXIV governing free trade areas. Thus, the "bilateral-track" provisions—those safeguarding against serious injury from surges in Canada–United States trade due to the agreement— last only through the ten-year phase-in period. Their innovation is an ambiguous definition of temporariness.[21] The "global-track" provisions—those safeguarding against all other sources of serious injury—are essentially just reaffirmations of GATT article XIX rights and procedures. The FTA's innovations are: (1) that either partner will be excluded from a global safeguarding action if its share in the other partner's market is small enough (less than 5 percent, or maybe 10 percent); (2) that when included in a global safeguarding action, neither partner's exports will fall below a trend line that allows for growth; and (3) that disputes over safeguarding actions are ultimately subject to binding arbitration.

These provisions suffer from several shortcomings.

First, because they are based on GATT article XIX, they do not distinguish between immobile resources, which are clearly most vulnerable to injury from the adjustment pressures associated with trade liberalization, and mobile resources, which are less vulnerable. The latter include, most notably, multinational corporate capital, which is discussed below.

Second, in providing safeguards under current procedures, governments lack the means to ensure that such protection decreases over time; they are frequently not able to resist powerful interest groups, nor therefore to establish credibility in asserting that such measures are temporary, nor therefore to encourage positive adjustment. This shortcoming is also discussed below.

Finally, the imprecision of chapter 11's language may jeopardize the preferential treatment that the United States and Canada grant each other under the FTA's global safeguard provisions. Exclusion from global safeguarding (innovation 1) might be construed strictly as exclusion from a formal article XIX initiative, measured, for example, by notification of all GATT trading partners.[22] Formal article XIX initiatives, however, are increasingly rare, having been supplanted by informal alternatives, such as "voluntary" restraint arrangements (VRAs). Canada–U.S. relations have been notably free of VRAs,[23] and Canadian trade officials believe that chapter 11 provides adequate means to resist them in the future. Yet, it is not clear how the United States would react in a situation of extraordinary sectoral pressure.[24] Conceivably, U.S. officials could argue that FTA article 1102 does not explicitly cover VRAs. In this case, the United States might resist the otherwise novel commitment to binding arbitration (innovation (2)). Finally, the provision for each partner's exports to be maintained under global safeguarding at a "trend . . . over a reasonable recent base period with allowance for growth" is tantamount to a selective VRA in the context of an otherwise nondiscriminatory global action. Thus, innovation 2 virtually invites the kind of grudging negotiation (What base period is "reasonable"? Do "growth" rates have to be positive numbers?) that frequently gives birth to any VRA.[25]

Overall, the safeguard provisions need strengthening. Given more time or opportunity, a restructuring of safeguards might have vitiated the rancorous fixation of pressure groups and negotiators on unfair trade remedies, which have been used increasingly along with VRAs as imperfect substitutes for safeguards.[26] Some suggestions for restructuring are made in the final part of this essay.

Growing Mobility of Corporate Capital and the Adjustment Climate for the Immobile

An important question in these regards is whether traditional adjustment policies and safeguard practices are adequate or appropriate anymore, in the face of growing international mobility of corporate capital and the corresponding amplification of unforeseen pressure on immobile workers and resource owners.

As firms have grown multinationally over the past few decades, the mobility of corporate capital—equipment, technology, and skilled personnel—has grown apace. Mobility of large, multinational firms and their professional work force internationalizes ostensibly domestic policies, amplifying their spillover surges abroad and provoking foreign adjustment. There is, of course, always *some* tendency for a country's sectoral policies, for example, to spill over abroad in mirror-image fashion. But the size of these spillover surges is much larger when corporate capital is mobile. Alert multinationals may decide that their expansion can be shifted to whichever of their affiliates enjoys the most favorable sectoral policy incentives. Technically "domestic" subsidies and taxes can thus easily become instruments of strategic sectoral predation among countries, predation that is often without any malicious intent, but that nevertheless can impose serious injury on the corresponding sector abroad.[27]

It is no surprise that as multinational corporate size and strategic influence have increased, subsidies, performance requirements, and unfair trade have become hard bones of contention in the policy environment.[28] The recent claim that strategically calculating policy can shape ("create," "destroy") a country's comparative advantage is correct, after all, where that same policy is capable of moving capital endowments from one country to another, using the mediating facilities of internationally coordinated firms, and leaving labor and immobile endowments behind.

Much the same could be said about active regional policy, and for similar reasons. The FTA, in fact, lubricates the mobility underlying these concerns in its provisions for easier temporary migration of businesspersons, engineers, architects, management consultants, and specified other professionals.

These changes have aggravated the potentially injurious stimuli prodding workers, farmers, landlords, local firms, and other owners of immobile resources. Moving the goods and moving the plant across borders are close substitutes to a large multinational firm—but not to its immobile workers and their unions and communities. Displaced workers, midlevel managers, and locally rooted entrepreneurs who are unable to acquire or transfer skills useful to alternative sectors face long periods of unemployment and below-average earnings.

In brief, immobile workers and resource owners seem to be saddled with sharper and more frequent unforeseen shocks from international forces than they were in the past.[29] Some of the agents who represent them are strategically large within countries, although uncoordinated across them, such as unions, regional governments, and departments (ministries) of agriculture. Their lack of coordination accentuates the unpredictability of spillover surges of competitive products and resultant injury. Their large size invites strategic interaction between them and their national government that can lead to indefinite protection—a kind of strategic paralysis of unproductivity that is the antithesis of successful adjustment or safeguard policy.[30]

In this environment, the challenge to policy is formidable. Adjustment burdens can be reduced if policy minimizes the economic hardship to immobile segments of the population, and sensible policy may include temporary and degressive protection. But commitment to eventual adjustment seems a necessity, since rational strategic agents will forecast government action when contemplating a specialized investment.[31] Government commitment to "preservation" makes zero private adjustment the strategic and equilibrium response. Government commitment to unspecified "eventual" adjustment makes waiting the strategic and equilibrium response. Only credible commitment to adjustment makes it possible for government to alleviate injury, while anticipation of the end of this alleviation alters ex ante location and allocation decisions in such a way that injury and the need for relief shrink. The challenge is to structure the policy to avoid "injury dependency" and the creation of addicts best described as the "injured underclass"!

In these regards, general adjustment programs and the bilateral-track provisions of the FTA are encouraging. Adjustment programs in both Canada and the United States emphasize training, retraining, and mobility much more, and unconditional income support much less, than they once did.[32] Safeguard restoration of trade barriers due to bilateral injury can be granted for three years only, without renewal, for any good. But the global-track safeguard provisions are unimaginative, and the (indefinite?) exclusion of certain products—including logs, unprocessed fish, and beer—from full FTA obligation is equivalent to a permanent safeguard.[33]

The agreement may yet provide opportunity for a more thorough restructuring of adjustment programs, especially for safeguards, with potential for mutually reinforcing progress on subsidies. In the next section, we turn to several ideas for such restructuring.

TWO IDEAS FOR SAFEGUARD RESTRUCTURING

In light of the environmental shifts and safeguard inadequacies discussed above, Canada and the United States should undertake negotiations on adjustment pressures and policy provisions to cope with them. General adjustment programs in each country are reasonably respected, so the discussion should focus primarily on safeguards only. Meetings might profitably track those regarding subsidies, both because subsidies often accentuate adjustment pressures, as argued above, and because joint progress on adjustment policy should make each country more tolerant of subsidies that would fall between "permitted" and "prohibited" categories in the subsidies discipline as Gary Horlick and Debra Steger suggest in chapter 4.

"Domestic Producers" Are the Immobile

Bilateral-track safeguards are explicitly available to a "domestic industry"; global-track (article XIX) safeguards are explicitly available to "domestic producers." These terms are traditionally interpreted as denoting the firms and workers making a product that is being pressured unexpectedly by a competitive foreign substitute. Yet, growing diversification of large firms across boundaries and products makes the notion of unforeseen serious injury to *them* much less compelling than it used to be, and the notion of unforeseen serious injury to their workers and small suppliers much more compelling.[34] It is perhaps timely to conceive of workers, small firms, communities, and immobile resource owners as the truly *domestic* producers of "like or directly competitive goods," in the words of the GATT (article XIX). Large firms, by contrast, and all owners of mobile capital are perhaps better conceived as *multinational* producers of *many* products. As such, they are already self-insured against the serious injury that safeguards are designated to avoid.

Narrowing the conception of domestic producers to workers, small firms,[35] and the immobile is the underlying foundation of the recommendations of the Economic Council of Canada and of extensive policy analysis by Robert Lawrence and Robert Litan for the United States.[36] Such narrowing could have several advantages in a renegotiated safeguard system. It might reduce the calculated magnitude of serious injury, and thus also the burden of ensuing safeguard protection. Or, if not, since injury to the immobile may be amplified, a narrower conception would at least refine the way serious injury is diagnosed, reducing the attention to profits and increasing the attention to employment as indicators that are typically monitored in domestic administration of safeguards.[37] Finally, a narrower conception might suggest a natural and appealing link between revenue from safeguard tariffs or auction quotas and required adjustment. Such revenue could be used to provide small-business reorientation, severance bonuses for workers, support to their pension programs (for example, for early retirement), or subsidies for retraining or relocation.[38] Earmarking safeguard revenue to encourage adjustment in this way would raise the likelihood that a safeguard really is temporary, and implicitly compensate foreign suppliers by "making space" for them in the domestic product market.[39]

Large firms and industry groups would not lose out entirely. They would presumably still be able to petition for safeguard relief under the narrower definition of domestic producers, and would still realize benefits from temporary protection. Yet, they would need to establish their safeguard case by demonstrating serious injury to their workers, small suppliers, and communities, not to themselves. Large firms' ability to tap the system for indefinite rents would be limited by the targeting of revenues toward worker exit and the corresponding difficulty in making any case for renewed and continuing safeguards.[40]

Coordination via an Arms-length Agent

It is hard for a national government on its own to guarantee credibly that safeguard protection is only temporary or degressive. In an extreme example, when the serious injury that justified the protection continues to exist, the domestic incentives make it irresistible for the government to repeat its "temporary" dose at similar intensity—and to repeat it again and again. Strategically rational agents, who sense how irresistible this pattern is, will refuse to believe in the proclaimed temporariness of the trade policy, and will remain active in the protected sector rather than leave it. Their continued activity keeps conditions the same as those that warranted the safeguard in the first place, and seduces the government into repeating its policy of temporary protection. The sequence then repeats itself. It should be clear that this cycle represents a strategic equilibrium, a position of rest in which temporary or degressive safeguards are impossible (that is, not sustained by the postulated strategic behavior).[41]

Strategic coordination among governments can help break this cycle by lending credibility to a government's pledge that a safeguard will be temporary or degressive. A joint affirmation alone can help, such as is provided in the bilateral track of the agreement, covering number of years, rate of degressivity, ability to repeat, allowable repetition interval, and so forth.[42] It gives a government ability to resist otherwise legitimate pressure from its constituents, and signals resolve to agents protected by safeguards, prompting them to adjust more and to lobby less.

Even more credibility and adjustment would be attained if a binational arms-length agent monitored and ultimately helped manage bilateral adjustment burdens and safeguard actions. Such an agent would facilitate international pressure on the two national governments to keep degressivity credible to domestic constituents.[43]

Insertion of a representative arms-length agent into safeguard actions would have both informational and strategic benefits. These benefits would have the character of a "public good," accruing to each country individually without depriving or exploiting the other. Thus, each government could claim to be a constituent of an arms-length agent out of unabashed national self-interest. Modeling and forecasting, monitoring and surveillance, would be among the agent's functions. Its membership and staff presumably would represent both Canada and the United States, yet be insulated to some degree from procedural pressures. It should be a standing committee, presumably an adjunct of the Canada–United States Trade Commission,[44] composed of an equal number of knowledgeable officials appointed by each government and supported by appropriate technical expertise. When either government considered safeguard actions affecting the other—for example, following a finding of injury by the International Trade Commission or the Canadian International Trade Tribunal—it could provide analyses of alternative measures. When one party notified the other of its intention to implement a safeguard action affecting the other, the committee could provide analyses of proposed actions and, if requested, advisory opinions to aid the consultations required by article 1102.

The informational benefits that an arms-length agent would provide spring from two sources. One is the need for common empirical understanding to allow governments to reach any agreement at all on the propriety of safeguards or impending pressures for them. The second is the need every government has to evaluate inherently opaque administrative substitutes for safeguards, not only abroad but even at home.

The strategic benefits of an arms-length agent would spring initially from its informational benefits.[45] Each national government should be better able to resist inappropriate domestic pressure for safeguard protection against bilateral trade if it can appeal to objective, widely available data and forecasts that belie the appropriateness of a safeguard. Each national government should also be better able to resist deflections of injury into its own market from unwarranted safeguard substitutes that its bilateral partner pursues with third countries.[46]

NOTES

1. The Economic Council of Canada calls these "framework policies." See Economic Council of Canada, *Managing Adjustment: Policies for Trade-Sensitive Industries* (Ottawa, 1988); and _____, *Adjustment Policies for Trade Sensitive Industries* (Ottawa, 1988).

2. I discuss this perspective in more detail for the broader context of the General Agreement on Tariffs and Trade (GATT) negotiations. See J. David Richardson, "Safeguards Issues in the Uruguay Round and Beyond," in Robert E. Baldwin and J. David Richardson, eds., *Issues in the Uruguay Round* (Cambridge, Mass.: National Bureau of Economic Research, 1988).

3. The following works are especially useful for surveying various studies of sector-by-sector adjustment pressures: Peter Morici, "The Canada–U.S. Free Trade Agreement," *International Trade Journal* 3, no. 4 (Summer 1989), pp. 347–373. Sunder Magun and Someshwar Rao, "An Assessment of the Economic Impact of the Canada–U.S. Free Trade Agreement," presented at the North American Economics and Finance Association, New York, December 28–30, 1988 (updating Economic Council of Canada, *Venturing Forth: An Assessment of the Canada–U.S. Trade Agreement* [Ottawa, 1988]); Paul Wonnacott, *The United States and Canada: The Quest for Free Trade, an Examination of Selected Issues,* Policy Analyses in International Economics, no. 16 (Washington, D.C.: Institute for International Economics, 1987); and Brian F. Shea, "The Canada–United States Free Trade Agreement: A Summary of Empirical Studies and an Industrial Profile of the Tariff Reductions," Economic Discussion Paper, no. 28 (Washington, D.C.: Department of Labor, Bureau of International Labor Affairs, 1988).

   The following are especially useful for surveying analyses of and experience with adjustment to all international trade shocks, whether due to trade liberalization or not: Economic Council of Canada, *Managing Adjustment;* _____, *Adjustment Policies;* G. E. Salembier, Andrew R. Moroz, and Frank Stone, *The Canadian Import File: Trade, Protection, and Adjustment* (Montreal: Institute for Research on Public Policy, 1987); and Ronald J. Wonnacott and Roderick Hill, *Canadian and U.S. Trade Adjustment Policies in a Bilateral Agreement* (Toronto and Washington, D.C.: Canadian-American Committee, 1987).

4. Noteworthy among them are Richard G. Lipsey and Murray G. Smith, *Global Imbalances and U.S. Policy Responses: A Canadian Perspective* (Toronto and Washington, D.C.: Canadian-American Committee, 1987); Peter Morici, *Reassessing American Competitiveness* (Washington, D.C.: National Planning Association, 1988); and _____, *Meeting the Competitive Challenge: Canada and the United States in the Global Economy* (Toronto and Washington, D.C.: Canadian-American Committee, 1988).

5. Drusilla K. Brown and Robert M. Stern, "Computable General Equilibrium Estimates of the Gains from U.S.–Canadian Trade Liberalization," presented at the Conference on Economic Aspects of Regional Trading Arrangements, Lehigh University, Bethlehem, Pennsylvania, May 25–27, 1988, University of Michigan Research Seminar in International Economics Discussion Paper, no. 220. Many alternative studies calculate estimates for Canada alone, not for the United States, and for industry employment and output alone, not for firm (plant) viability and market structure. See, for example, Magun and Rao, "Assessment."

6. Offsetting this are important strengths. The underlying empirical representation allows for economies of scale and industry rationalization in a much more judicious and varied way than alternative studies do. For example, Brown and Stern realistically divide industries into those with firms that are perfect and imperfect competitors, into those characterized by free entry and others, and into those facing global markets and those facing only national markets. In addition to this richer array of realistic market structure, Brown and Stern shun the much-criticized "focal pricing" assumptions that have characterized many alternative models, but that have little behavioral foundation or empirical support.

7. Many commentators believe that the Free Trade Agreement creates mostly intra-industry pressure. See, for example, Murray G. Smith, "What is at Stake?" in William Diebold, Jr., ed., *Bilateralism, Multilateralism and Canada in U.S. Trade Policy* (Cambridge, Mass.: Ballinger for the Council on Foreign Relations, 1988), p. 74; and Economic Council of Canada, *Adjustment Policies*, pp. 19–20.

8. Brown and Stern discuss the technical difference between their approach and others. Morici, in "The Canada–U.S. Free Trade Agreement," provides a table with the same disaggregation as Table 1, comparing the estimated Canadian employment effects among the Brown and Stern study, the Magun and Rao study, and industry studies conducted under the auspices of the Royal Commission on the Economic Union and Development Prospects for Canada (the Macdonald Royal Commission). During 1989, Canada's Department of Industry, Science, and Technology began releasing industry studies of the effects of the Free Trade Agreement for a finer disaggregation, with 119 sectors featured. As a rule, all the studies generate similar rank orderings of industries along a continuum from strong gainers to unfortunate losers (leather products, printing and publishing, and chemicals are the exceptions, with ranks that differ significantly across the various studies). Despite similar rankings, the Brown and Stern study calculates proportionately larger amplitudes of percentage gains and losses than the others.

9. This is shown in the table, in that the U.S. figures are roughly one-tenth the Canadian; it is important to keep in mind that 1 percent of the U.S. labor force is roughly ten times the size of 1 percent of the Canadian labor force.

10. According to numerous accounts, the Canadian business community has pursued all three kinds of diversification.

11. Economic Council of Canada, *Adjustment Policies*.

12. Canadian service sectors are estimated to grow uniformly in both output and jobs, and U.S. service sectors to shrink, but these results would probably be less significant if the agreement's services liberalization had been captured.

13. Magun and Rao, "Assessment"; and Richard G. Harris and Victoria Kwakwa, "The 1988 Canada–United States Free Trade Agreement: A Dynamic General Equilibrium Evaluation of the Transition Effects," presented at an NBER/CEPR Conference on Strategic Trade Policy, University of Sussex, England, July 8–9, 1988.

14. Magun and Rao predict that the productivity gain would boost aggregate employment as well as wages. While this prediction is controversial, it is more likely in the short run (when adjustment pressures are highest) than in the long run. Brown and Stern, by contrast, assume the FTA has no effect on aggregate employment.

15. See also the calculations of normal exit, entry, and turnover in Economic Council of Canada, *Adjustment Policies*, pp. 11–35. These are not, however, lined up against adjustment pressures from the FTA, as they are in Harris and Kwakwa, "The 1988 Canada–United States Free Trade Agreement."

16. Morici, in chapter 1 of this volume, notes the danger that these macroeconomic adjustment pressures may be blamed directly on the FTA itself.

17. For lengthy descriptions of these policies in Canada, see the Economic Council of Canada, *Adjustment Policies;* and A. Jean de Grandpre, *Adjusting to Win*, report of the Advisory Committee to the Government of Canada on Adjustment (Ottawa: Ministry of Supply and Services, 1989), appendix D. For U.S. policies, see Charles F. Stone, "International Trade," in Isabel V. Sawhill, ed., *Challenge to Leadership: Economic and Social Issues for the Next Decade* (Washington, D.C.: Urban Institute Press), pp. 128–135.

18. See Economic Council of Canada, *Adjustment Policies;* and de Grandpre, *Adjusting to Win*.

19. For Canada, see de Grandpre, *Adjusting to Win*. For the United States, see "New Direction in Trade Policy: Changes in the Law," *AFL–CIO News*, August 13, 1988, p. 4.

20. Both still have limited programs of special adjustment assistance for "trade-impacted" workers. But these programs are much smaller than in the 1960s and 1970s in both countries, as funding for them has been reallotted toward adjustment assistance for all structurally unemployed workers, without regard to cause. De Grandpre, *Adjusting to Win*, pp. 36–38, defends this shift in emphasis.

21. Any good can benefit from a bilateral-track safeguard only once, and for no more than three years, in contrast to the GATT's vague "for such time as may be necessary to prevent or remedy such injury." After the ten-year phase-in period, however, new bilateral safeguards are permissible only "by mutual agreement."

22. FTA article 1102 on global actions begins as follows: "With respect to an emergency action taken by a Party on a global basis, the Parties shall retain their rights and obligations under article XIX of the General Agreement on Tariffs and Trade." The rest of the article refers to "such action" or "action authorized under paragraph 1."

23. Canadian cooperation during U.S. negotiation of steel VRAs is possibly the only exception, with a potential U.S. safeguard action lurking as the background threat, since Canada was neither dumping nor subsidizing its exports.

24. An example might be nonferrous metals in the next U.S. recession.

25. In addition to encouraging selective VRAs, albeit in *favor* of each party to the agreement, the safeguarding provisions have several dubious features. They explicitly mandate compensation, while many commentators favor abandoning it in global safeguard reform, so as to avoid its tendency to discourage recourse to GATT article XIX. (See Richardson, "Safeguard Issues," pp. 26–27.) They define and use the word "surge"—normally associated with the concept of market disruption under the Multifibre Arrangement, but judiciously skirted in safeguard discussions to avoid invidious comparisons. And they fail to require "positive adjustment" by producers as a precondition for being granted safeguard relief, as recommended by GATT reformers. See Fritz Leutweiler et al., *Trade Policies for a Better Future: Proposals for Action* (Geneva: General Agreement on Tariffs and Trade, 1985); and recently written into U.S. domestic safeguard legislation (section 201 of the Trade Act, as revised in the Omnibus Trade Bill of 1988).

26. Richardson, "Safeguard Issues," pp. 28–30; and Andreas F. Lowenfeld, "Fair or Unfair Trade: Does It Matter?" *Cornell International Law Journal* 13 (Summer 1980), pp. 205–219.

27. The focus in the discussion is on how the movement of large, multinational firms of any nationality can heighten adjustment pressure on smaller, immobile domestic firms and factors. The Economic Council of Canada, by contrast, is concerned with nationality, not mobility—with whether Canadian firms differ from non-Canadian multinationals operating in Canada (see its *Adjustment Policies*, ch. 4). The international mobility of *Canadian* multinationals can, however, be a significant source of adjustment pressure on immobile Canadians, and appears to be taking place. See Alan Freeman, "Free Trade Pact Creates Winners, Losers: Canadian Firms Forced to Adjust Their Operations," *The Wall Street Journal*, February 7, 1989, p. A16.

28. Miriam Camps and William Diebold, Jr., illustrate this when they write that "one of the basic principles that we think should guide the new multilateralism . . . [is] that the international community has a legitimate concern with domestic actions when they have important external effects." See their *New Multilateralism: Can the World Trading System Be Saved?* (New York: Council on Foreign Relations, 1983), p. 22.

29. Gene M. Grossman and J. David Richardson, *Issues and Options for U.S. Trade Policy in the 1980s: Some Research Perspectives* (Cambridge, Mass.: National Bureau of Economic Research, 1982).

80 □ MAKING FREE TRADE WORK

30. On these grounds, governments themselves could support the data-gathering and information-dissemination functions of the independent agency recommended in the next section. It could free them from the unwelcome political pressure of the large constituencies who might have and should have taken prudent steps earlier if only they had been informed—for example, they might have moved, stayed in school, or gone to vocational classes instead of the night shift of the endangered local employer. Generally, in fact, the agreement can be faulted for inadequate provision for regular reports, updates, forecasts, and public relations.

31. Economic Council of Canada, *Adjustment Policies,* pp. 10–13, includes an attractive summary of these matters under the headings "specificity of labour skills and capital equipment" and "anticipated vs. unanticipated change."

32. The Canadian Advisory Committee on Adjustment plays down income maintenance and recommends training and retraining by firms themselves for their own workers, which, if adequate, relieves them from a special payroll tax to finance government adjustment programs. See A. Jean de Grandpre, testimony before the Standing Senate Committee on Foreign Affairs, Senate of Canada, December 29, 1988, in *Third Proceedings,* 1988, pp. 3.53–3.77; and _____, *Adjusting to Win.* A number of reasons justify thinking that firms can administer and monitor training programs more efficiently than the government. In the United States, safeguard income support for trade-displaced workers and firms now depends on the drafting of an acceptable adjustment plan; merely demonstrating injury is no longer sufficient.

33. In March 1989, the United States began a section 301 counteraction in the case of unprocessed fish on the grounds that Canada's export ban was an unfair trade barrier; the United States won a GATT ruling to that effect in 1988.

34. Risk-taking owners and managers of large, interrelated stocks of capital are presumably better informed than workers and the petite bourgeoisie about prospects for international change, and also about finding more lucrative employment of their resources by moving to other industries. They therefore have more opportunities than workers and other small agents to diversify. Large firms are supported (or confronted) by financial intermediaries with multinational scope or contacts who are presumably even better informed than the large firms about international and interindustry prospects.

35. Defining "small" firms or, more precisely, "immobile" firms would be one of the first practical tasks of negotiations over these changes. That it is not an impossible task can be seen in the successful adjustment of the size threshold at which the Canadian government reserves the right to review U.S. takeovers of Canadian firms.

36. Economic Council of Canada, *Adjustment Policies,* pp. 113–114; and Robert Z. Lawrence, and Robert E. Litan, *Saving Free Trade: A Pragmatic Approach* (Washington, D.C.: Brookings Institution, 1986).

37. Robert E. Baldwin, *The Political Economy of U.S. Import Policy* (Cambridge, Mass.: MIT Press, 1985), ch. 3.

38. These are very close in spirit to the recommendations of the Economic Council of Canada (see *Managing Adjustment* and *Adjustment Policies*) and the Advisory Committee on Adjustment (see de Grandpre, testimony and *Adjusting to Win*).

39. Lawrence and Litan, in *Saving Free Trade*, recommend that explicit compensation to foreign suppliers comes out of the earmarked revenue. Ultimately, this might be feasible between countries as close as Canada and the United States.

40. Wonnacott and Hill, in *Canadian and U.S. Adjustment Policies*, p. xiv, point out a further possible advantage of excluding large firms from direct safeguard relief. Such relief is arguably an industrial subsidy under some circumstances and might provoke agitation for countervailing initiatives (within the same sector, and hence despite any compensation).

41. The policy problem is known technically as time inconsistency: this year's optimal value for next year's policy intensity will no longer look optimal when next year rolls around, once private strategic reaction to the policy is taken into account. The same problem can afflict all temporary policy. The evidence for it, however, is in reality mixed. The evidence seems strongly supportive in some industries and countries (textiles and apparel, steel, footwear in Canada) and not supportive in others (televisions, U.S. footwear). On the relatively good record of the United States in keeping safeguards and safeguard substitutes temporary and often degressive, see Robert Z. Lawrence and Paula DeMasi, "The Adjustment Experience of Escape Clause Relief," in Gary Clyde Hufbauer and Howard F. Rosen, *Trade Policies for Troubled Industries*, Policy Analysis for International Economics, no. 15 (Washington, D.C.: Institute for International Economics, 1986); Robert Z. Lawrence, "A Depressed View of Policies for Depressed Industries," presented at the Conference on U.S.–Canadian Trade and Investment Relations with Japan, Ann Arbor, Michigan, April 2–3, 1987, pp. 10–13; and Gary Clyde Hufbauer, Diane T. Berliner, and Kimberly Ann Elliott, *Trade Protection in the United States: 31 Case Studies* (Washington, D.C.: Institute for International Economics, 1986); and Vinod K. Aggarwal, Robert O. Keohane, and David B. Yoffie, "The Dynamics of Negotiated Protectionism," *American Political Science Review* 81 (1987), pp. 345–366. On the less successful record of Canada, see the descriptions of special import measures for footwear, textiles and clothing, and automobiles in Economic Council of Canada, *Adjustment Policies*, ch. 5; the discussion of sectoral subsidies in pulp and paper and in shipbuilding also illustrate the problem (ibid., ch. 6).

42. Thomas Dorsey has pointed out that the notion of credible degressivity almost forces tax-based safeguards, either safeguard surtariffs or voluntary export taxes administered by the trading partners of a safeguarding importer. (One advantage of the latter would be that domestic political pressures on the exporter would generally work strongly to guarantee degressivity and temporariness.) Credible degressivity is much more difficult to conceive for quantitative barriers. Unlike safeguard taxes, they translate into variable rates of protection as economic conditions change. Degressivity cannot even be defined without forecasts of those conditions—forecasts that will be wrong at least half the time in a direction that

makes quantitative safeguards inadequately degressive. In this light, the little-used Canadian safeguard surtaxes have much to recommend them, and the more frequently employed global quotas have less appeal, even though endorsed by the Economic Council of Canada (see its *Adjustment Policies*, pp. 53–54 and 114–117).

43. The reasoning is the same that underlies the quasi-independence of a central bank from political forces, and that accords the International Monetary Fund or a new intermediary an independent role in helping debtors' promises appear credible to creditors.

44. Frank Stone very early suggested a similar structure, and outlined considerable detail regarding authority, responsibility, membership, and so on. See Frank Stone, "Institutional Provisions and Form of the Proposed Canada–United States Trade Agreement," Discussion Paper in International Economics, no. 8604 (Montreal: Institute for Research on Public Policy, 1986). For similar proposals, see also Economic Council of Canada, *Adjustment Policies*, p. 115; and, with regard to subsidies, chapter 4 of this volume.

45. Indeed, these are what the Economic Council of Canada stresses above other benefits. See *Adjustment Policies*, pp. 114–115 and 117–118.

46. A more radical set of strategic benefits might evolve if, in time, the mandate of the arms-length agent were extended to reviewing all national safeguard protection, and publicly evaluating its appropriateness, in the fashion of a standing version of the binational panels for unfair trade remedies. This would, of course, require the negotiation of acceptable definitions of terms such as "domestic producers" (immobile resources?) and "emergency" (degressivity?), and procedures for appeal, dispute settlement, access to the proceedings, and so on. Still more radical (and hence distant) evolution might involve a representative safeguard committee, with ability to remand safeguard decisions to national authorities, and ultimately perhaps to supplant them in hearing and determining safeguard cases.

FOR FURTHER READING

Canada. "The Canada–U.S. Free Trade Agreement: Synopsis." December 1987.

Frankel, Jeffrey A. "The Sources of Disagreement among the International Macro Models and Implications for Policy Coordination." Working Paper, no. 1925. Cambridge, Mass.: National Bureau of Economic Research, 1986.

Frankel, Jeffrey A., and Katharine Rockett. "International Macroeconomic Policy Coordination when Policymakers Do Not Agree on the True Model." *American Economic Review* 78 (June 1988), pp. 318–340.

Grignon, Louis, and Kei Moray. "Geographic Labour Mobility in Canada." Working Paper, no. 88-1. Ottawa: Economic Studies and Policy Analysis Division, Fiscal Policy and Economic Analysis Branch, Department of Finance, Government of Canada, 1988.

Hufbauer, Gary Clyde, and Howard F. Rosen. *Domestic Adjustment and International Trade*. Washington, D.C.: Institute for International Economics, 1989.

Lipsey, Richard G., and Murray Smith. "More FTAs: Implications for Canada's Trade Strategies." Presented at the conference More Free Trade Areas?, Institute for International Economics, Washington, D.C., October 31–November 1, 1988.

Lipsey, Robert E., and Irving B. Kravis. "Is the U.S. a Spendthrift Nation?" Working Paper, no. 2274. Cambridge, Mass.: National Bureau of Economic Research, 1987.

Little, Jane Sneddon. "At Stake in the U.S.–Canada Free Trade Agreement: Modest Gains or a Significant Setback." *New England Economic Review* (May/June 1988), pp. 3–20.

Morici, Peter. "The Canadian–U.S. Free Trade Agreement: Origins, Contents, and Prospects." Presented at the Conference on Economic Aspects of Regional Trading Arrangements, Lehigh University, Bethlehem, Pennsylvania, May 25–27, 1988.

Mundell, Robert A. "International Trade and Factor Mobility." *American Economic Review* 47 (June 1957), pp. 321–335.

Mutti, John. *U.S. Adjustment Policies in Trade-Impacted Industries*. Washington, D.C.: National Planning Association, 1985.

Organization for Economic Cooperation and Development. *Structural Adjustment and Economic Performance*. Paris, 1987.

———. *Historical Statistics, 1960–85*. Paris, 1987.

Richardson, J. David. "Empirical Research on Trade Liberalization with Imperfect Competition: A Survey." *OECD Economic Studies* 12 (Spring 1989), pp. 7–50.

Stern, Robert M., Philip H. Trezise, and John Whalley, eds. *Perspectives on a U.S.–Canadian Free Trade Agreement*. Washington, D.C.: Brookings Institution, 1987.

United States Department of Commerce, International Trade Administration. "Summary of the U.S.–Canada Free Trade Agreements." Washington, D.C., 1988

World Bank. *World Development Report*. New York: Oxford University Press for the World Bank, 1988.

4

SUBSIDIES AND COUNTERVAILING DUTIES

Gary N. Horlick & Debra P. Steger

The problem of subsidies and their discipline has bedeviled trade negotiations and policymakers for almost twenty years.[1] It was not surprising to most observers that Canadian and U.S. negotiators were unable to resolve these difficult issues in the recent negotiation of the Canada–U.S. Free Trade Agreement (FTA).

The negotiators attempted to resolve the subsidy and countervailing duty issue by seeking agreement on new binational rules and mechanisms governing the use of subsidies.[2] However, the subject proved too difficult and politically contentious to resolve in the last few months of the negotiations.

Instead, the two countries agreed to establish a working group to continue these negotiations over the next five to seven years. In the interim, they agreed to establish binational panels to rule on whether new countervailing duty legislation proposed by either country violates the FTA, the General Agreement on Tariffs and Trade (GATT), or the GATT subsidies code; and to establish binational panels to review final countervailing duty determinations.[3] The first procedure should restrain the development of new trade barriers masquerading as countervailing duty amendments on either side of the border. The second should provide for expedited review of determinations by domestic agencies. It also addresses the problem of a perceived lack of confidence in the fairness of the domestic systems. The establishment of a working group is a practical accommodation to both the political opponents of going too far too fast and the inherently complicated and technical nature of the issues.

The mandate of the working group, as set out in the FTA, is to "seek to develop more effective rules and disciplines concerning the use of government subsidies," and to "seek to develop a substitute system of rules dealing with unfair pricing and subsidization." It is required to report to the two governments "as soon as possible," and both countries have agreed to "use their best efforts to develop and implement the substitute system of rules" within five years (this period may be extended for a further two years if the two governments wish).[4]

THE PROBLEM

As tariffs decline in any liberalized trade regime, the relative effects of other trade distortions become more significant.[5] Thus, there is a widespread concern that the continued use of subsidies and the current unfair trade laws in both countries could undermine the gains the FTA will make in eliminating tariffs and reducing nontariff barriers. However, the dimensions of the problem may have been overstated, both during the negotiations and in the popular press.

Both countries subsidize a wide range of business activity. However, few subsidies are large enough to attract countervailing duty actions in either country. Although there have been relatively few countervailing duty cases in either country involving imports from the other; most of the cases have been brought in the United States against Canadian goods.[6] Not surprisingly, given the structure of trade and the levels of subsidization, the majority of countervailing duty cases between Canada and the United States have involved resource and agricultural products (for example, corn, pork, fish, raspberries, and lumber).[7]

The first task for the working group should be to develop a comprehensive inventory of subsidies in both countries. In addition, accurate statistics should be compiled on the amount of cross-border trade in each allegedly subsidized industry. Only by determining the parameters of the problem can the negotiators seek to develop appropriate rules to deal with it.

The relative levels of subsidization in the two countries are only part of the problem. From an exporting country's point of view,[8] a major difficulty is the threat of harassment to its exporters from the use of countervailing duty laws. Also, for several reasons, countervailing duty cases are often an expensive, burdensome, and inefficient means to discipline the use of trade-distorting subsidies.

First, a countervailing duty regime penalizes subsidized goods in the importing country, but does nothing to reduce harmful effects of subsidies in third-country markets or the economy of the subsidizing country. For example, a U.S. countervailing duty imposed on imports of a subsidized product from Canada will not necessarily lead to the cessation of the subsidy practice. It will not remedy the injury the subsidy has caused in other U.S. export markets, such as Europe, or in the Canadian economy. This is the major difference between a countervailing duty system and a true subsidy discipline regime. Whereas a countervailing duty system can only authorize tit-for-tat retaliation on imports of subsidized products, a subsidy discipline regime can deal up front with the harmful effects of subsidies in the world economy at large.

Second, countervailing duties are a relatively ineffective means of disciplining potentially trade-distorting subsidies. For example, a capital assistance grant of 10 percent of the value of a new plant in a capital-intensive industry would be subject, in most cases, to a countervailing duty of less than 1 percent on the value of current production. Because countervailing duties usually are calculated for a whole industry (which may include unsubsidized firms), it becomes apparent why the assessment of duties in U.S. cases involving Canadian regional development subsidies has always been below 1 percent of the export price of the goods.

Third, economists are dubious about whether it is rational for a country to restrain subsidized imports that may bring gains to its economy as a whole even though competing domestic producers may suffer somewhat in the bargain. Some economists argue that subsidized imports may actually improve welfare in the importing country while creating negative effects in the exporting country and the world economy as a whole.[9]

Furthermore, countervailing duties levied in most U.S. cases involving Canadian imports have been low, because the total subsidy amounts have been relatively small.[10] Generally speaking, once a government grant is allocated over total sales and amortized over the appropriate useful life, the resulting subsidy is small. Thus, a successful petitioning industry often does not obtain a significant tariff benefit, and the subsidized exporter may ultimately be faced with a rate of duty that is not a major impediment to trade.

Finally, countervailing duty cases are costly, for the domestic and foreign industries involved and for their governments.[11] Defending a countervailing duty case, for example, can easily cost more than U.S. $200,000 in the United States or Cdn. $125,000 in Canada in legal fees alone. Even more expensive are the demands on company executives' and government officials' time, particularly in a prolonged dispute. The horror stories are the cases like softwood lumber, which probably cost $6–$8 million in legal fees and even more in high-level executive time. That case also involved a great deal of government time, at both the federal and the state or provincial levels.

Perhaps the most significant cost of countervailing duty cases is the chilling effect they have on new investment. The uncertainty and unpredictability of the current domestic systems also creates serious difficulties for policy development, particularly for Canada, which is heavily dependent upon international trade.

A PROPOSAL

Countervailing duty laws alone are not the answer to reducing the incidence and the adverse effects of trade-distorting subsidies. What, then, are the options?

The first option would be to agree to an up-front discipline on all subsidies—that is, to prohibit them. Clearly, such a solution would not be politically feasible and might not be economically desirable. Not all subsidies have trade-distorting effects, and governments often use them for socially beneficial, public policy objectives.

A second option would be to develop a set of rules and to establish an independent, supranational level of government to govern subsidies within the free trade area. That is, in effect, what the European Community (EC) has done under article 92 of the Treaty of Rome. The idea of establishing a supranational agency to administer subsidy rules—with the authority ultimately to roll back trade-distorting government programs—would not be politically acceptable to either the United States or Canada.

In our view, the subsidy and countervailing duty dilemma has no simple or obvious solutions. We propose a hybrid regime, consisting of new principles for the discipline of subsidies, binational administrative procedures for the initiation and determination of complaints, and a revised role for domestic countervailing duty laws.

Agreeing to new principles concerning subsidies discipline would fulfill two important objectives. First, it would promote the general goal of trade liberalization by reducing and inhibiting the use of government subsidies as trade-distorting (including import-substituting) devices. Second, it would provide guidelines to both governments and businesses in selecting permissible types of support when planning new programs in the future. The only sure way to guarantee certainty and predictability (as well as freedom from harassment) in any new system is to develop a common set of principles for subsidies discipline.

The most likely approach is an agreement listing specific types of "permissible" and "prohibited" forms of government assistance.[12] Ideally, prohibited subsidies would be defined as programs with a *direct* effect on bilateral trade—including, in the broadest sense, import substitution and displacement of exports to third-country markets, as well as the more classic injury to producers in the importing country. Permissible programs would be those with, at most, an *indirect* or *negligible* effect on bilateral trade. Because the precise trade effects of domestic—that is, nonexport—subsidies are difficult to measure, a simple, workable methodology for classifying government programs should be developed and built into the agreement.

In specifying the list of prohibited subsidies, the negotiators should start with the kinds of programs that have been generally agreed as having trade-distorting effects—for example, export subsidies and financial assistance that directly affect export performance. A useful first step would be to adopt the Illustrative List of Export Subsidies that appears as an Annex to the GATT Subsidies Code. In addition to the general prohibition of export subsidies on nonprimary products in the Subsidies Code, the FTA obligates the two governments to refrain from using export subsidies on agricultural products traded bilaterally. There would seem to be clear a priori agreement, therefore, to include those export subsidies on the prohibited list.

The permissible category would certainly include the widely used social programs that both countries have. A primary political imperative, from Canada's point of view, would be to assert early on in the negotiations that these programs—including medicare, unemployment insurance, education, social security, and certain other health and safety programs—are permissible.[13]

An interesting question is whether it would be useful (and, indeed, possible) to list certain other types of programs, with specific parameters and conditions, as permissible. These could include, for example, some general research and development (R&D), national security, environmental, employee training, adjustment assistance, and cultural programs. "Permissibility" for these categories would be limited to programs that generally create positive externalities (ideally, on both sides of the border, such as some R&D or joint defense programs) and do not distort cross-border trade. Although the negotiation would be difficult, Canadian regional development programs and U.S. state and municipal programs could conceivably be listed in the permissible category, where they do no more than offset the additional costs for firms of locating in a depressed area. The scope of such additional costs and formulas for computing them would have to be spelled out in the agreement.

The benefit of having a common set of rules is that it would establish a class of government programs (the permissible category) that would always be free from complaint or challenge. It would also establish a class of prohibited forms of government assistance, which could be dealt with expeditiously and strictly in a binational system. A third category of government programs, those falling in between, would be dealt with in a transparent, binational system.

We would anticipate that for political reasons the initial lists of permissible and prohibited subsidies would be fairly short. Most types of domestic subsidies would undoubtedly fall into a middle ground—a gray area. Recognizing that perfect solutions will never emerge in an imperfect world, but also wanting to eliminate the uncertainties endemic in the current system, we would recommend a very simple, basic procedure to discipline trade-distorting, domestic subsidies that do not appear on the prohibited or permissible lists. The basic rule for subsidies in the gray area would be that any *direct* government financial assistance to businesses (even if nonspecific)—such as grants, loans, equity investments, tax credits, or tax forgiveness—totaling more than a negotiated percentage (x percent) of capital costs or of operating expenses would be prohibited.[14] Likewise, any programs involving a direct transfer of financial assistance from government to private firms *below* x percent of capital costs or of operating expenses would be free from challenge.[15] Any deviations from these general rules could be met by fairly harsh retaliatory actions. This would leave behind a residual group of alleged indirect government assistance programs, including such politically "hot" items as infrastructure and availability of natural resources to a specific industry. As discussed below, these would be subject to the applicable, revised, domestic countervailing duty procedures, which would include an injury test.

Transparency and Dispute Settlement

In order for a subsidy discipline regime to operate smoothly, it must have transparency (that is, each country must be informed of the other's programs) and acceptable procedures for settling disputes. For the reasons stated earlier, it is our view that creating independent, authoritative supranational institutions, like the EC, is not politically feasible in the Canada–U.S. free trade area. We think that there is merit in building upon the experience of both countries with the GATT, the FTA, and their own domestic systems.

To establish a binational monitoring or surveillance mechanism, Canada and the United States should be required to notify
each other of all existing and proposed programs, preferably
through a joint committee that would be established under the
FTA. This committee should be a permanent investigative body
composed of highly qualified officials, an equal number from
each government, who are responsible within their respective
capitals for administering the FTA. The committee would have
ongoing responsibilities to review existing and proposed government programs and to analyze their effects on bilateral trade.[16]

Binational panels (those created under either chapter 19 or
chapter 18 of the FTA) could be directed to perform two new
tasks: reviewing any proposed program (federal or subnational)
that the committee believes may have adverse direct effects on
trade, and reviewing any complaints about existing programs.

Binational Review of Proposed Programs

Each government should be required to notify the other
(through the committee) of any proposed national or subnational government program. The committee would conduct an
independent analysis of the proposed program, and if it was of
the opinion that the program was in the prohibited category or
otherwise might have a direct effect on bilateral trade, it could
request the establishment of a binational panel to provide an
advisory opinion.

The procedures could be similar to those in article 1903 of
the FTA, dealing with review of amendments to countervailing
duty laws. As in the latter case, these procedures should include
opportunities for government-to-government consultations, reference to a panel if no solution is found within a specified period
of time, opportunities for negotiations after a panel has ren-
dered its advisory opinion, and the ultimate sanction of compensation or retaliation where the opinion is not implemented.

Enforcement

Given that industries in Canada and the United States have
private access to countervailing duty procedures, it would not be
feasible to limit their rights to initiate proceedings.[17] To the

contrary, private petitions would be useful as a means of both defusing import-restrictive pressures and enforcing the subsidy rules.

We would recommend maintaining the existing domestic procedures whereby producers can petition or complain about imports of subsidized products causing or threatening to cause injury to domestic industries, subject to some revisions[18] to reduce the number of unfounded actions. Such amendments might include the following:

- Permit (or require) consultations prior to the initiation of an investigation either between the investigating government agency and the foreign exporter or with the governments and the private industries involved in both countries (with safeguards to preclude antitrust problems). These consultations prior to initiation would help to improve understanding of the facts, to reduce misconceptions, and to encourage early resolution of cases. Several U.S. and Canadian business groups have expressed the view that some bilateral trade disputes could be resolved better by some form of alternative dispute resolution involving all parties *prior* to initiation of a formal investigation.

- Establish more rigorous standing requirements. A requirement that petitioners or complainants prove, for example, that 50 percent of the domestic industry supports a petition would reduce the number of cases initiated without the support of the majority of an industry.[19]

We would propose a major change in existing procedures at the next step in an investigation. All petitions or complaints would be referred, first, to the joint committee to determine whether they provide sufficient evidence on which to proceed and, second, to a binational panel for an advisory opinion on the question of the effects of the subsidy. The tasks of the committee and the binational panel will be relatively simple if the subsidy complained of falls into a designated permissible category: the case would stop there. In a clear-cut case, the committee could determine that the program was permissible and submit its decision for ratification by a panel. Even if a panel's finding is not technically "binding," it would be referred to the domestic investigating agency, which would normally cease the investigation.

Where a binational panel finds that a program falls into the prohibited category or that a direct subsidy falling in the gray area violates the x percent rule, the offending government should be given a specified time to remove the program. If that country does not comply within the designated time, the other government should be able to apply to the binational panel for authorization to take equivalent retaliatory action until the program is removed. This retaliatory action in effect would be like a countervailing duty without an injury test—except that the duty would not only cover subsidized imports, but would also be calculated to take into account the impact of import substitution in the subsidizing country and third-country effects of the subsidy.[20]

Where a binational panel finds that the program complained of does not fit into either the permissible or the prohibited category, and is not a form of direct assistance subject to the x percent rule, it would determine whether the program is an actionable subsidy under the applicable domestic countervailing duty law, quantify its amount, and refer the case to the domestic agency responsible for conducting an injury inquiry.[21] The case would then proceed as a domestic countervailing duty investigation, subject to a number of suggested improvements.

We would recommend that a new bilateral system include the following changes in domestic countervailing duty procedures:

- Establish a more rigorous standard of material injury ("injury") at the preliminary determination stage. The current U.S. standard—the presence of a "reasonable indication" that a domestic industry is materially injured or threatened with material injury—is extremely loose. Similarly in Canada, the Canadian International Trade Tribunal (CITT) does not make a preliminary review of injury unless specifically requested, and the investigation continues unless a very limited inquiry by the Department of Revenue, Customs and Excise fails to disclose any evidence of injury. Consequently, most injury determinations at the preliminary stage are affirmative. Requiring a more rigorous injury standard at the preliminary stage, such as "more probable than not" or "substantial," could eliminate unwarranted petitions early.

- In cases where third-country or import-substitution effects are not seriously at issue, require x percent market penetration by the complained of imports in assessing injury at the preliminary stage. Since reasonably accurate market penetration statistics are almost always available at the time of the preliminary injury determination, proceedings in which U.S. or Canadian imports have only an insignificant market share could be terminated before substantial costs are incurred.

- Require U.S. or Canadian products under investigation to amount to x percent of all imports of that product from all countries subject to investigation as a prerequisite to a finding of injury at the preliminary stage. Again, since accurate import statistics are usually available at the preliminary injury determination stage, early termination would be encouraged in cases where U.S. or Canadian imports represent only a small fraction of all imports.[22]

- Exclude imports from the other country from the cumulation provision[23] unless (1) Canadian or U.S. exporters are the principal exporters of the product under investigation, or (2) Canadian or U.S. exports, in and of themselves, cause injury.

- Ensure that the majority of the domestic industry is injured by requiring that 50 percent of domestic producers (in a large industry, 50 percent of a representative sample) respond to the questionnaires issued by the CITT or, in the United States, the International Trade Commission. This requirement could be imposed at the preliminary (or final) injury determination stage. If 50 percent of the domestic industry is unwilling to take the time to respond adequately to the questionnaires, the exporters from the other country should not be required to sacrifice further executive time or incur additional expenses to defend themselves in a countervailing duty proceeding.

• Require that a direct causal link be proved between any injury actually suffered by or threatened to a domestic industry and the subsidization. This could be done either by requiring proof that the subsidization was a "significant"— not just "any"—cause of injury, or by imposing a duty only to the extent necessary to offset the injury caused by the subsidization.[24]

OBSTACLES

One theoretical obstacle to an agreement to discipline domestic (that is, non-export-contingent) subsidies is that the United States has less motive to agree to such a regime than Canada. In fact, some officials involved in the free trade negotiations have indicated that it was the United States, not Canada, that balked in the final days of the negotiations at making any commitments with respect to the granting of subsidies.[25] This can be illustrated by an extreme example—what may be called the five-to-one problem. Let us suppose that Canada and the United States each produce one tradeable good, and each country subsidizes that one good. Let us further assume that the United States exports 10 percent of its tradeable good to Canada, and Canada exports 50 percent of its tradeable good to the United States. Canada would be five times as willing to give up its subsidies on 100 percent of its tradeable in return for security of market access for 50 percent of that good than the United States would be to give up subsidies on 100 percent of its tradeable to guarantee market access for 10 percent.

Similarly, the requirement to demonstrate injury before countervailing duties are levied on direct subsidies falling in the gray area has a contrary effect on the larger market's incentives to discipline the use of subsidies. Specifically, since market share is used as an indicator of injury, *ceteris paribus,* the larger country may find that its exports into the smaller market are subject to countervailing duties more often than are the small country's exports into the larger market.[26]

The role of third-country subsidy practices may have asymmetric implications for the large and small countries, depending upon the market structure and pattern of trade barriers in an industry. Where Canada and the United States are selling fungible commodities in offshore markets, they may both be reluctant to control subsidy practices on a bilateral basis and instead may prefer multilateral disciplines.[27] However, for differentiated manufacturing products sold in more segmented markets, the small country may attach higher priority to obtaining secure access to the larger market, while the large country may attach a higher priority to multilateral disciplines.

It is somewhat ironic that the United States may have less theoretical reason to discipline domestic subsidies than Canada. The free trade negotiators seem to have realized this, although the political debate in both countries has been based on the assumption that the United States would be *more* willing than Canada to accept disciplines on its domestic subsidies.

The political obstacles would appear to be more problematic than the theoretical ones. U.S. congressmen have demanded that Canada be forced to reduce its subsidies, but the United States has not examined what it is willing to give up. Meanwhile, some Canadian politicians seem to equate the ability to subsidize freely (that is, to transfer money from average taxpayers to businesses) with the Canadian national character.

These various obstacles may cancel each other out. The U.S. political demands for disciplines on subsidies could be assuaged ultimately by an adequate, but less-than-perfect discipline on Canadian subsidies. Also, a less-than-perfect discipline on U.S. subsidies would likely be more politically palatable in the United States than the more rigorous versions that U.S. politicians and negotiators sometimes espouse. At the same time, a less-than-perfect discipline on subsidies would enable Canadian politicians to claim that essential sovereignty had been preserved and would help both countries to meet their deficit reduction goals.

Even if the obstacles ultimately prevent an overall agreement on subsidies and countervailing duties, the bilateral working group would provide a timely opportunity for both countries to address a worthwhile goal of mutual benefit—the limitation or elimination of "locational" subsidies. These are the packages of incentives that are assembled, typically by states or provinces, to lure a new plant to a particular locale. Bidding wars often develop among the treasuries of states and provinces (as well as local governments) to attract the same plant (often built by foreign manufacturers). Different subnational governments within one country may compete against each other (for example, Kentucky against Kansas for a new Toyota plant). A bidding war across the U.S.–Canada border may result in a trade dispute, with the loser complaining that the winner had an unfair advantage (for example, Nova Scotia against Ohio for a Michelin tire plant).

States and provinces usually cannot forswear locational incentives unilaterally, without risking the loss of new plants to competing subnational governments. However, if all U.S. states and Canadian provinces and the two federal governments agreed not to offer (or to limit) such incentives, no one government would be disadvantaged.[28]

CONCLUSION

Given all the obstacles, is a bilateral agreement on subsidies discipline negotiable within the next five to seven years? We are cautiously optimistic that an agreement can be achieved. Some of the preliminary work has already been done, and the GATT multilateral negotiations on subsidies may help to build consensus (at least between Canada and the United States) on the difficult, definitional issues. The key to success would be a realization by the working group and its political masters that "three-quarters of a loaf is better than none." For obvious reasons, neither government will be willing to forswear all domestic subsidies. Consequently, any agreement on subsidies would likely result in a limitation on their use, rather than their complete elimination. Seeking precise definitions of those limits will tax the creativity of the members of the working group.

Although we would encourage the negotiators to aim high, and make every effort to negotiate a comprehensive set of principles and methodologies that would resolve the definitional uncertainties and ambiguities relating to the discipline of subsidies, pragmatism leads us to predict that this goal may not be achievable in the short term.

Thus, we have proposed a hybrid system based on certain new bilateral rules and disciplines, and designed to build on the experience of the two countries with their domestic countervailing duty systems, chapter 19 of the FTA, and the GATT. Ultimately, we think, a binational system for enforcement of subsidies discipline is essential in a free trade area. Limitations on the use of subsidies would imply corresponding limitations on the application of countervailing duties. The resolution of those two related problems would remove one of the most contentious issues between the United States and Canada in recent years.

NOTES

1. John H. Jackson considers subsidies the most difficult problem in international trade. See John H. Jackson, "Achieving a Balance in International Trade," *International Business Lawyer* 14, no. 4 (April 1986), pp. 123–128; see also Gary C. Hufbauer, "Subsidies Issues after the Tokyo Round," in William Cline, ed., *Trade Policy in the 1980s* (Washington, D.C.: Institute for International Economics, 1983), pp. 327–362.

2. A primary objective of the government of Canada in requesting the free trade negotiations in 1985 was to limit the ability of the United States to impose countervailing duties on Canadian imports. Canadian negotiators, however, realized that any negotiation with the United States about countervailing measures could not be attempted without also negotiating disciplines on subsidies.

3. Chapter 19 of the FTA includes antidumping as well as countervailing duty laws; however, antidumping is outside the scope of this paper.

4. Articles 1906 and 1907.

5. Hufbauer, "Subsidies Issues," p. 327.

6. From 1980 to 1989, there were fifteen U.S. countervailing duty cases initiated against Canadian products, and only one Canadian case against U.S. products (U.S. grain corn).

7. In the nonagricultural sector, subsidies are lower than many people realize. Two recent studies prepared for the Institute for Research on Public Policy in Ottawa indicate that in the industrial sector, subsidies average less than 1 percent of the value of production. See Andrew R. Moroz, *Grant Support and Trade Protection for Canadian Industries*, Working Paper, no. 8801 (Ottawa: Institute for Research on Public Policy, 1989); and Ira Kaminow, *Current Subsidy Estimates of Selected U.S. Production Subsidies*, Working Paper, no. 8802 (Ottawa: Institute for Research on Public Policy, 1989).

8. As noted above, Canadians have been the defendants in all but one U.S./ Canadian countervailing duty case to date. In the only Canadian case against the United States, the defendant (the National Corn Growers Association) complained bitterly about being embroiled in a countervailing duty case, and obtained authority for the secretary of agriculture to reimburse up to $500,000 for its legal expenses. See Omnibus Trade and Competitiveness Act of 1988, section 4304(b).

9. See Robert M. Stern, ed., *U.S. Trade Policies in a Changing World Economy* (Cambridge, Mass.: MIT Press, 1987).

10. In the five U.S. cases involving imports from Canada that have received preliminary or final determinations since 1980, the subsidies found have ranged from less than 1 percent (oil country tubular goods and raspberries) to 15 percent (softwood lumber, in 1986). Most have been small—for example, 5.82 percent (for groundfish), 1.47 percent (for fresh flowers), less than 1 percent (for swine). The notable exception was the 1986 softwood lumber case. The only Canadian countervailing duty case brought against the United States to date, involving imports of grain corn, was also exceptional. The subsidies found in that case amounted to approximately 67 percent of the value of the U.S. imports. See *Oil Country Tubular Goods*, 51 Fed. Reg. 15,037 (1986) (Final); *Certain Red Raspberries from Canada*, 50 Fed. Reg. 47,124 (1985) (Final); *Certain Fresh Atlantic Groundfish*, 51 Fed. Reg. 10,041 (1986) (Final); *Fresh Cut Flowers from Canada*, 52 Fed. Reg. 2,134 (1987) (Final); *Softwood Lumber from Canada*, 51 Fed. Reg. 37,453 (1986) (Prelim.); and Revenue Canada, *Final Determination on Subsidized Grain Corn from the United States of America* (Ottawa: 1987).

11. The U.S. and Canadian governments spend substantial sums conducting these investigations. Query: Might the governments' funds not be better spent directly on assisting petitioning industries in improving their competitiveness rather than on investigating a multitude of programs that result in only insignificant countervailing duties? For example, in the raspberries cases, the U.S. petitioners, after two administrative proceedings (an antidumping and a countervailing duty investigation), court actions, and a subsequent administrative proceeding, obtained a 2.41 percent dumping margin and only a 0.99 percent countervailing duty rate. See *Certain Red Raspberries from Canada*, 50 Fed. Reg. 47,124 (1985) (CVD, Final), 50 Fed. Reg. 26,638 (1985) (AD, Final); ITC Inv. Nos. 701-TA-254 and 731-TA-196, USITC Pubs. 1743 and 1658 (1985). The cost to the U.S. government of conducting these investigations must have exceeded $100,000, in addition to the costs of defending the litigation. Ironically, the International Trade Commission's record contained a great deal of information about the U.S. industry's pressing need to increase its marketing efforts—efforts that may have required less expenditure than the trade cases. Government funds available on a generic basis to assist companies in marketing their products could benefit *both* countries' industries without differential trade effects. See University of Oregon, "Study of Competitiveness of U.S. Producers," in respondents' brief, on file at the U.S. International Trade Commission.

12. Much of this work was done during the 1985–1987 negotiations.

13. Oddly enough, no one seems to have contemplated the likely fate of any U.S. elected official who agreed to cut back or limit, through an international agreement, U.S. programs such as Social Security.

14. If this cannot be done on a general basis, the working group might negotiate different thresholds for specified industries.

15. This already occurs, as no countervailing duties are charged below a *de minimis* level of 0.5 percent in the United States. Any such threshold is likely to be the subject of intense negotiations.

16. It would not be necessary to establish an entirely new, independent agency to administer the subsidy rules. Officials from the existing government departments responsible for administration of the FTA could be directed to perform these responsibilities.

17. In the United States, in particular, the opposition to such a proposal likely would be fierce. The trend in Canada has been increasingly to open up a previously secretive, discretionary government process to provide producers with rights to initiate proceedings, requiring, *inter alia,* public hearings as well as reasoned, published decisions. In the 1988 Canadian International Trade Tribunal Act, for example, Canadian producers were given new rights to initiate safeguard investigations.

18. This obviously would entail establishing a special set of countervailing duty laws and procedures (a bilateral track) for goods traded bilaterally, as distinct from the laws and procedures applied to goods from third countries. Creating a bilateral track for countervailing duty procedures would be within the ambit of article XXIV of the GATT. Article XXIV releases contracting parties who have created a free trade area from their most-favored-nation obligations under the GATT, provided that "the duties and other regulations of commerce maintained in each of the constituent territories and applicable at the formation of such free trade area . . . to the trade of contracting parties not included in such area . . . shall not be higher or more restrictive than the corresponding duties and other regulations of commerce existing in the same constituent territories prior to the formation of the free trade area," article XXIV:5(b).

    Interpreted literally, article XXIV:5 states that the normal GATT obligations do not apply to the countries forming a free trade area where they have not made their existing "duties and other regulations of commerce" vis-à-vis third countries more restrictive than the corresponding regulations in force prior to the establishment of the free trade area. In our view, the term "other regulations of commerce" is broad enough to include countervailing duty laws. By changing the domestic countervailing duty laws as they apply to the other member of the free trade area, the laws that apply to third countries after the formation of the free trade area have not been made more restrictive than they were prior to the formation of the free trade area. The laws and procedures applicable to third countries have, in fact, remained the same. For a comprehensive examination of this question, see Michael M. Hart, "GATT Article XXIV and Canada–United States Trade Negotiations," *Review of International Business Law* 1 (1987), pp. 317–355.

19. The antidumping code and the U.S. definition of "industry" require that injury be assessed against a "major proportion" of producers. Canadian

and U.S. law has typically found, in practice, that 20–40 percent is sufficient to constitute a "major proportion."

20. Canada would be unlikely to accept a limitation to "traditional" countervailing duties, under which the United States could countervail the approximately 76 percent of Canadian exports sold to the United States while Canada could reach only the approximately 22 percent of U.S. exports destined for Canada. Conversely, U.S. negotiators may insist that these third-country or import-substitution effects be given less weight than direct export effects.

21. In the United States, it would be referred to the International Trade Commission, and in Canada, to the Canadian International Trade Tribunal.

22. Article 1102 of the FTA, dealing with global safeguard actions, includes similar provisions. It requires that U.S. or Canadian imports be excluded from a global action unless such imports are substantial (that is, in the range of 5–10 percent or more of total imports) and are contributing importantly to the injury caused or threatened by all imports.

23. The cumulation provision (required in U.S. law and practiced in most cases in Canada) authorizes the investigating agency to assess together the volume and price effect of imports of the same or substantially similar products from all countries. Thus, Canadian or U.S. imports may be included in a proceeding even though the real dispute is with exports from a third country.

24. Although it is not an explicit requirement, the GATT subsidies code suggests that a countervailing duty need not be greater than necessary to remedy the injury caused. U.S. law requires that a duty be imposed in the amount of the subsidy. In Canadian law, as a result of the public interest provisions, it is possible for the minister of finance to adjust a duty to an amount less than the subsidy.

25. M. Peter McPherson, deputy secretary of the treasury, speech at conference on the Canada–U.S. Free Trade Agreement, cosponsored by the Institute for International Economics and the Institute for Research on Public Policy, Washington, D.C., January 11, 1988.

26. Thus, the United States has a larger share of the Canadian market than vice versa in at least two product areas where U.S. industries have brought countervailing duty cases (steel and fish). Nonetheless, the imposition of countervailing duties will impose less of a burden upon production in the large country.

27. Agricultural trade is an obvious example. Both countries recognized this in article 701 of the FTA, where they agreed to prohibit export subsidies and to work together in the Uruguay Round to develop new multilateral disciplines concerning domestic, agricultural subsidies.

28. It can be argued that disadvantaged states or provinces need to be able to offer incentives to compete with more desirable locations. To the extent that this is true, and desirable, it should be considered in the negotiation of permissible regional development programs.

5

THE IMPACT OF THE AGREEMENT ON MEXICO

Sidney Weintraub

The central thesis of this essay is that the operations of the Canada–U.S. Free Trade Agreement (FTA) will, over time, bring progressively increasing pressure on Mexico to make some accommodation to the FTA in its trade policy. The ability to work out an accommodation of some sort (what this might mean is discussed later) is now possible because of the remarkable opening in the Mexican economy during the past several years. In the short term, modification of Mexican policy in response to the FTA is unlikely to result in a North American free trade area (NAFTA) encompassing the three countries, or in a Mexico–U.S. free trade agreement, but measures will be necessary to protect growing Mexican exports of manufactures to the North American market, especially to the United States. The possibility of a NAFTA or a separate Mexico–U.S. free trade agreement in the long term will depend on the pace and extent of Mexican economic recovery, the success of the FTA in stimulating U.S.–Canadian trade and investment, the degree of trade liberalization achieved in the Uruguay Round of negotiations in the General Agreement on Tariffs and Trade (GATT), and the degree of trade diversion that Mexico experiences because of the FTA.

THE MEXICAN TRADE SITUATION

During the six-year term of President Miguel de la Madrid (December 1, 1982, to December 1, 1988), Mexico made a fundamental change in its trade policy from high protection and looking inward for markets for manufactured goods to reduced protection and a drive to promote manufactured exports. The

102

Mexican tariff level before the change was not a significant measure of protection, because nontariff measures were dominant, particularly the requirement for import licenses. By the end of the de la Madrid administration, about 6 percent of the more than 8,200 items in Mexico's import structure were subject to licensing; in value terms, however, licensing still affected some 20 percent of imports.[1] Mexico is seeking to unify its import tariff at 20 percent. The simple average is now around 10 percent, and the trade-weighted average about 6 percent. Mexico's tariffs are still not as low as those of the United States, the European Community (EC), or Japan, but they are approaching that league. (The trade-weighted U.S. tariff is 3 percent. The United States, however, has more tariffs at or above 20 percent, especially for textiles and footwear, than Mexico.) While Mexico's nontariff protection is still high, as evidenced by the remaining 300 items subject to the prior licensing requirement, the economy is no longer closed.

The motive for the trade opening, and the corollary measures taken in the industrial and financial areas, was to promote exports of manufactured goods. The collapse of the old structure of development from within became evident when oil prices fell in 1981, and then even more clear when oil prices fell again in 1986. Oil exports in 1985 had been $14.8 billion; they dropped to $6.3 billion in 1986. Oil amounted to almost 70 percent of total exports in 1985, and less than 40 percent of the total in 1986 (see Figure 1). Total exports between those two years fell by more than $5.5 billion. Mexico's payments on its external debt, meanwhile, were still substantial—about 6–7 percent of gross domestic product (GDP) and 30–35 percent of exports of goods and services—and this limited the country's options (see Figure 2). If a significant part of Mexico's interest payments were not to be withheld, exports other than oil were needed. And under these circumstances there was, and still is, no alternative to increasing manufactured exports.

Mexico took several measures to augment nonoil exports: the peso was devalued to make it somewhat undervalued with respect to the U.S. dollar, funds for export financing were in-

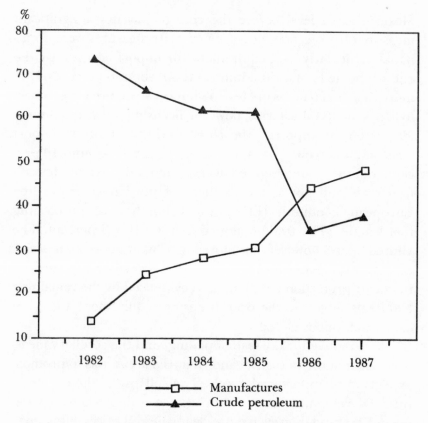

Source: Banco de México, *Indicadores Económicos,* December 1988.

FIG. 1. MEXICO'S EXPORTS OF CRUDE PETROLEUM AND MANUFAC-
TURES AS PERCENTAGE OF TOTAL EXPORTS, 1982–1987

creased; and industrial subsidies were used more selectively in
the interest of efficiency rather than protection.[2] As stated in a
report by one of Mexico's leading banks, the main guidelines of
the country's new model are to promote exports, open the economy, reduce the size of the public sector, use subsidies more
sparingly, and link the financial and productive sectors to ensure
that the latter has adequate credit.[3]

The use of labels can oversimplify, but it is clear that Mexican economic policy, at least as it affects the structure of industry
and foreign trade, has become more neoclassical and less struc-
turalist in the sense that the latter word has been used in Latin
America. The export pessimism that accompanied the struc-

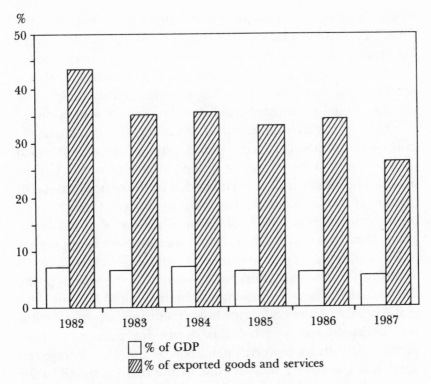

%

Source: Banco de México, *Indicadores Económicos, December 1988.*

FIG. 2. MEXICO'S INTEREST PAYMENTS ON EXTERNAL DEBT
AS PERCENTAGE OF GDP AND PERCENTAGE OF EXPORT
GOODS AND SERVICES, 1982–1987

turalist approach of the Economic Commission for Latin America from the 1950s well into the 1970s—the emphasis on import substitution as the way to break the dependency of the periphery on the core—has given way in Mexico to an emphasis on the essentiality of exports. The policy has not met universal acceptance in Mexico. Many economists and political figures still see the development model as requiring heavy state intervention and reliance on the domestic market.[4]

The economic opening involves primary reliance on a price-dominated model—employing modest tariffs rather than licensing, imposing fewer domestic and export subsidies, and using the exchange rate as an instrument of trade and financial policy—rather than the regulated model that so thoroughly dominated the Mexican economy for most of the period since the 1930s. The philosophic gulf between the two perceptions—market versus regulatory dominance—is deep, and the reconciliation may be a long time in coming. The earlier model was jettisoned because its failure was evident by the 1980s. The current model presumably requires success if it is to endure.[5]

One of the driving impulses of earlier Mexican economic policy—in addition to the philosophic concepts discussed above—was to achieve greater independence from the United States. This desire is deeply embedded in the official psyche of Mexico. It is reflected in the emphasis in Mexican foreign policy on nonintervention in the affairs of other states. It partly explains Mexican votes in international organizations in opposition to U.S. positions. Year in and year out, Mexico—at least as much as any other noncommunist nation—votes on the side opposite the United States on key resolutions in the United Nations General Assembly. Mexico's foreign investment and import-substitution policies have reflected this desire for maximum independence from its powerful neighbor. When Mexico rejected entry into the GATT in 1980, one of the reasons stated in the literature of the period was that because the United States dominated the GATT, entry would increase U.S. influence over Mexico's trade policy.

The neoclassical dominance in current foreign economic policy reflects a downgrading—not overtly stated, but implicit—of Mexico's effort to distance itself from the United States. Mexico did join the GATT in 1986. It has concluded a number of bilateral arrangements with the United States—on subsidies and countervailing duties, and on procedures for accelerated negotiation on issues of concern to either or both countries. Mexican officials have suggested the idea of sector agreements with the United States, although the content of such agreements remains vague.[6] Reliance on price rather than regulation also implies finding one's markets and one's sources of imports through means other than official dictation.

In 1987, $13.3 billion of Mexico's exports—64 percent of the total $20.7 billion—went to the United States. For manufactures, the proportion going to the United States was around 80 percent.[7] Even this understates the reliance on the United States. The value added in Mexican *maquiladora* exports was $1.6 billion in 1987, which represented largely value added (mostly labor) in manufacturing enterprises.[8] These exports are recorded not in Mexico's trade figures, but rather in "transformation" services (that is, transforming goods into a more processed form by adding value) in Mexico's official balance-of-payments presentation.

In other words, the success of Mexico's new trade and industrial policies—if development is to be export-driven to the extent contemplated—hinges on continuing and growing dependence on the U.S. market. Industrial efficiency, to the extent that it develops in Mexico, should permit penetration of many markets; but for the foreseeable future, the crucial external market— indeed, the only crucial foreign market—is the United States.

The Mexican trade *apertura* (opening) took place in an atmosphere of circumstantial duress and was based on the need to generate a trade surplus, despite declining foreign-exchange earnings from oil exports, in order to pay interest on the external debt. The willingness to conclude bilateral trade agreements with the United States—actions that would have been an anathema a decade earlier—was an admission by the responsible authorities that trade dependency was less onerous than economic (and undoubtedly political) collapse. These outcomes were not foreordained. Other models could have been—or still can be—chosen, particularly if Mexican officials decide to limit payments on external debt.[9]

The question thus arises whether the new Salinas administration will continue the policies introduced during the *sexenio* (six-year term) of President de la Madrid. These policies include not just trade liberalization, but also the shrinking of the state sector, the maintenance of an undervalued (or at least competitive) exchange rate, and the welcome to foreign direct investment. The expectation is that Salinas will continue in these respects. His early actions during his first year as president support this probability. As secretary of programming and budget in the de la Madrid administration, Salinas had a large say in formulating his predecessor's policies. The new cabinet-level officers in the economic positions are technicians—largely with doctorates in economics from prestigious U.S. universities. They tend to view policy with an emphasis on efficiency rather than on political ideology.

But certain forces might impel changes in policy despite the desire for continuation. The most critical is the lack of growth in Mexico's economy for the last six years. Since this decline occurred as the new policies were put into effect, there is a *post hoc, ergo propter hoc* tendency to blame the economic disaster on those policies—the trade opening, the push to export in order to service external debt, and the shift from a state-dominated to a more private-sector-oriented economic model. The short-term political imperative to restore economic growth may take precedence over the long-term structure of the economy. The trade liberalization is leading to increased imports of consumer goods, most of which were excluded under the 1988 import-licensing system, and this is stimulating pressures for a return to more protection.[10] The need to combat inflation led to an appreciation of the peso in 1988 and into 1989; if this trend continues, the export-led growth model would be compromised.

And, perhaps most important, U.S. economic measures and performance will have great influence on Mexican policy. Inadequate relief from the burden of interest payments on external debt could force the Salinas government to take unilateral action. For Salinas in the short term, being seen to act to restore economic growth undoubtedly has political priority over maintaining good relations with the United States. An increase in U.S. and world interest rates would hit Mexico quite hard. Because of the combination of export-led growth and great reliance on the U.S. market, any faltering in the U.S. economy would have a severe impact on Mexico.[11] Growing U.S. protectionism poses great danger that Mexico would be prevented from effectively pursuing its present policy.

To the extent that future trade policy is under the control of Salinas's new economic team, the probability is quite high that the practices introduced during the de la Madrid administration will continue and even be augmented. But a number of imponderables—internal in Mexico, and external, particularly in the United States—could alter this conclusion.

MEXICO AND CANADA: SIMILARITIES AND DIFFERENCES

The most important trade similarity between Mexico and Canada is their great reliance on the U.S. market. In Canada's case, this dependence, coupled with fear of U.S. protectionism, was a major motivation for concluding a free trade agreement. Mexico has not yet been pushed that far, but the combination of dependence and protectionism did stimulate bilateral trade agreements with the United States and suggestions that the two countries might conclude sector agreements.

Mexico and Canada have other similarities. The dominant foreign investment position in both countries is from the United States. Each of them, consequently, has much trade between related parties (a parent and an affiliate, for example) in the United States and the respective country. For each, the most important financial connection—for credit, for exchange rate relationships—is with the United States. North America may not have a single economic unit, but there clearly are two closely connected relationships—Canada and Mexico, separately, with the United States.[12]

The differences between the two countries are substantial. Canada is a developed country; its annual per capita gross national product (GNP) is around U.S. $15,000. Mexico is a developing country, with a per capita GNP of about $1,800. Despite Canada's much smaller population (about 25 million, compared with about 80 million in Mexico), the U.S. market in Canada is four times that in Mexico (U.S. $59.8 billion, compared with $14.6 billion in 1987). U.S. imports from Canada are three-and-one-half times those from Mexico ($71.5 billion, compared with $20.5 billion in 1987). The current U.S. economic stake in Canada is vastly larger than that in Mexico, but the stake in more populous Mexico will surely one day rival or exceed that in Canada. The United States has a significant interest in seeing

Mexico converted into a source of economic dynamism in North America.

The economic differences between Mexico and Canada are important because they almost certainly preclude Mexican inclusion in a NAFTA for the time being. Canadians were concerned, as was evident in the electoral campaign that returned the Progressive Conservatives to office on November 21, 1988, that their country would be overwhelmed economically (and politically) in an FTA with the United States. Because of similar concerns, Mexican authorities have hardly even thought about the prospect of joining the United States in a free trade agreement, or entering a NAFTA.[13] Mexico has been searching for trading solutions (sector agreements of some sort, commodity-by-commodity negotiations) short of free trade with the United States.

Furthermore, many provisions in the Canada–U.S. FTA would be difficult—perhaps impossible—for Mexico to accept today. These include, but are not limited to, the pace of tariff dismantlement, the treatment of energy (especially oil), the derogation of sovereignty involved in the dispute settlement procedures, the proscribing of export performance requirements, and the virtual elimination of equity limits (except for the very largest companies) on foreign investment by U.S. nationals in Canada. Mexico's conversion from a state-regulated economy, looking inward, is too new to be pushed very far for now—to a free trade agreement with the very country whose dominant economic status it most fears. Exports in relation to GNP have long been more important to Canada than to Mexico (about a third, compared with roughly 15 percent). It will take time for Mexico to think in terms of free trade—of a NAFTA or a bilateral free trade agreement with the United States. Such an agreement may come—perhaps even in the next decade—but the relevant decisions for Mexico for now with respect to the Canada–U.S. FTA are different. These options are discussed below.

TRADE PRESSURES ON MEXICO

It is hard, a priori, to know what the trade-creating or trade-diverting effect of the Canada–U.S. FTA will be on Mexico.

Because of the small size of the Canadian economy compared with that of the United States (Canada's GNP is less than 8 percent that of the United States), the FTA is unlikely to stimulate much economic growth in the United States. (Canada has much more at stake in terms of potential added growth from the FTA.) Mexico, since its main export market is the United States, faces the potential of trade diversion from the FTA much more than the prospect of trade creation from U.S. participation in the agreement. Indeed, because of its need to increase exports of manufactured goods, coupled with its reliance on the U.S. market, Mexico is more vulnerable to trade diversion than any other country.

Table 1 shows the results of a partial attempt to anticipate the products in which diversion may occur. This effort entailed examining those products for which Mexico has an established market in the United States but faces competition from Canada. The sectors that have potential for market diversion are automotive, petrochemicals, iron and steel, other metals, paper products, textiles and apparel, and various items of machinery. Many of these sectors are highly protected in the United States by tariff and nontariff measures (for example, textiles and steel); consequently, the margin of preference that Canadian producers will have in the U.S. market under the FTA can be significant.[14]

It is not sufficient to look at products for which Mexico has an established market in the United States, because this excludes the growing competitiveness Mexico is achieving in other areas under its current trade and industrial policies. Table 2 does this for a limited group of products by looking at the twenty four-digit Standard International Trade Classification (SITC) manufactured products whose imports by the United States from Mexico increased most from 1985 to 1987. These were years of substantial growth of Mexico's manufactured exports. As Figure 1 shows, manufactures, which made up 30 percent of Mexico's exports in 1985, amounted to 48 percent of the total in 1987 (exceeding the share of oil, which was 38 percent in 1987). The sectors whose export growth stand out over this period include automotive, consumer durables (television receivers), furniture,

TABLE 1. U.S. IMPORTS OF MANUFACTURES EXCEEDING $20 MILLION
FROM MEXICO AND CANADA, *(value in millions of U.S. dollars,
and range of U.S. MFN tariff, 1987*[a])

SITC[bc]	Product	Mexico	Canada	Range of U.S. MFN tariff (%)[d]
5122	Alcohols, phenols, etc.	22	98	0–20
5133	Inorganic acids, etc.	61	69	0–4
5135	Metallic oxide for paint	25	51	na
5141–3	Metal composed of inorganic acid	34	140	0–17; median 3
5811	Product of condensation, etc.	43	99	0–12.5
5812	Product of polymerization, etc.	73	314	20[e]
6291	Rubber tires, tubes	38	530	0–5; median 4
6318	Wood simply worked, nes	60	70	0–5
6412	Other printing paper, nes	32	514	0–17; median 5
6419	Other paper, etc., nes, bulk	22	230	0–17; median 5
6429	Paper, etc., articles, nes	183	76	0–17; median 5
6516	Yarn of synthetic fibers	26	28	9–15; median 12
6569	Other textile products	70	41	0–30[e]
6612	Cement	157	159	0–$0.22/ton
6647	Safety glass	109	157	5–6
6651	Bottles, etc., of glass	23	39	6–38
6742	Iron, steel medium plate	36	247	6.5
6748	Iron, steel thin-coated, nes	54	133	6.5
6783	Iron, steel tube, pipe, nes	48	250	1–8
6811	Silver unworked, partly worked	277	123	0–6
6821	Copper alloys, unwrought	56	356	1–6
6822	Copper alloys, worked	45	88	1
6851	Lead, alloys unwrought	29	62	3.5 (on lead content)
6861	Zinc, alloys unwrought	42	302	2–19
6922	Mil transport boxes, etc.	23	37	0–6; median 5
6952	Tools, nes	24	55	4–8
6981	Locksmiths' wares	73	246	2–7.5; median 6
6986	Springs and leaves	36	187	4–6
6989	Other base metal manufactures	54	291	0–6

TABLE 1 *continued*

SITC^{bc}	Product	Mexico	Canada	Range of U.S. MFN tariff (%)^d
7115	Piston engines, nonair	973	1,639	0–4; median 3.7
7143	Statistical machines	150	477	na
7149	Office machines, nes	317	674	0–5; median 3.7
7184	Construction mining machinery, nes	30	225	0–3.7
7191	Heating, cooling equipment	124	132	2–4
7192	Pumps, centrifuges	103	291	0–3
7193	Mechanical handling equipment	76	262	0–6
7195	Powered tools, nes	25	81	2.5–4.5
7199	Machine parts, accessories, nes	64	330	0–6; median 4
7221	Electric power machinery	538	286	3
7222	Switchgear, etc.	516	313	5–6
7231	Insulated wire, cable	1,001	226	5–8; median 5.3
7241	Television receivers	293	32	6–15
7242	Radio broadcast receivers	604	15	4–8; median 5
7249	Telecommunications equipment, nes	813	567	5–8; median 5
7250	Domestic electric equipment	156	111	0–5
7291	Batteries, accumulators	56	30	5.1–5.3
7292	Electric lamps, bulbs	27	32	0–8; median 3.7
7293	Transistors, values, etc.	318	533	0
7294	Automotive electrical equipment	107	105	0–8; median 3
7295	Electrical measuring, control equipment	55	223	4–10; median near 10
7299	Other electrical machinery	299	193	3–5; median 4
7321	Passenger motor vehicles, except buses	1,178	10,257	2.5–8.5; median near 8.5
7323	Lorries, trucks	89	3,700	na
7328	Motor vehicle parts, nes	651	5,143	0–4; median 3
8124	Lighting equipment	38	27	0–8; median 3.7
8210	Furniture	311	1,031	2.5–9; median 6
8411	Textile clothes, not knit	307	96	median 17^e
8414	Clothing, accessories knit	66	35	above 20^e

TABLE 1 *continued*

SITC[bc]	Product	Mexico	Canada	Range of U.S. MFN tariff (%)[d]
8510	Footwear	105	35	2–48; median 37.5
8619	Measuring, controlling instruments	106	202	0–8; median 5
8912	Sound recording tapes, discs	74	57	4.2
8930	Articles of plastic, nes	80	555	2–14; median 5
8942	Toys, indoor games	88	27	0–12; median 7
8944	Outdoor sporting goods, nes	31	62	0
8960	Works of art, etc.	89	136	0–11; median near 11

Source: Data compiled from tapes of United Nations trade statistics; tariff and nontariff measures provided by U.S. Department of Commerce from U.S. International Trade Commission, *Harmonized Tariff Schedule of the United States*, 1st ed., supp. 3 (Washington, D.C.; United States Government Printing Office, 1988).

na = not applicable.

nes = not elsewhere specified.

[a] Manufactures are defined as Standard International Trade Classification (SITC) categories 5–8.

[b] It was necessary to translate SITC categories to the harmonized system (HS) now used for U.S. tariff purposes, and this is an inexact procedure. Hence, tariff ranges are shown. The conversions from SITC to HS are based on United Nations, *Standard International Trade Classification*, 3rd rev. (New York, 1986).

[c] The products in excess of $100 million exports are all produced primarily in the Federal District or the State of Mexico, with the exceptions of 7143 (Jalisco), 7191 (Nuevo Leon), 7293 (Jalisco), 7328 (Puebla), and 8510 (Jalisco). Of these exceptions, the Federal District and Mexico have the second-largest share of production for all items save 8510 (Guanajuato). These locational emphases reflect the dominance of the Federal District, Monterrey, and Guadalajara in Mexico's industrial production.

[d] Most numbers are rounded. The MFN tariff is that normally levied on imports from Mexico. This tariff will gradually decline to zero for imports from Canada.

[e] These are estimated ad valorem equivalents of mixed ad valorem and specific tariffs.

products of various metals, and clothing. Canada is a major supplier to the United States in most of these sectors.

Sectors in which Mexico has suggested that bilateral agreements might be discussed with the United States—for example, automotive products, petrochemicals, and textiles and apparel—tend to coincide with those sectors in which the Canada–U.S. FTA might divert exports from Mexico in favor of Canada. Mexico must make a more detailed examination of possible trade diversion than that undertaken here. However, the point to

TABLE 2. TWENTY MANUFACTURED PRODUCTS SHOWING GREATEST U.S. IMPORT GROWTH FROM MEXICO, 1985 AND 1987

		Value in ($000s)		Share		Average annual growth
SITC	Product	1985	1987	1985	1987	rate %
7321	Passenger motor vehicles, except buses	111,158	1,177,914	1.31	9.07	479.8
7241	Television receivers	88,147	292,655	1.04	2.25	116.0
7143	Statistical machines	6,109	149,962	0.07	1.16	1,177.4
7191	Heating, cooling equipment	29,905	124,080	0.35	0.96	157.5
7294	Automotive electrical equipment	27,254	106,915	0.32	0.82	146.1
7231	Insulated wire, cable	617,503	1,000,584	7.26	7.71	31.0
8210	Furniture	167,541	310,556	1.97	2.39	42.7
7192	Pumps, centrifuges	37,869	103,482	0.44	0.80	86.6
8617	Medical instruments, nes	46,842	109,841	0.55	0.85	67.2
6822	Copper, alloys worked	6,076	44,947	0.07	0.35	319.9
7250	Domestic electric equipment	80,807	156,497	0.95	1.21	46.8
6981	Locksmiths' wares	28,668	73,348	0.34	0.56	77.9
6291	Rubber tires, tubes	5,654	37,677	0.07	0.29	283.2
6748	Iron, steel thin-coated, nes	16,342	53,584	0.19	0.41	113.9
6821	Copper, alloys unwrought	18,933	55,580	0.22	0.43	96.8
6742	Iron, steel medium plate	7,803	35,852	0.09	0.28	179.7
8971	Real jewelry, gold, silver	26,312	64,058	0.31	0.49	71.7
6412	Other printing paper, nes	5,129	31,645	0.06	0.24	258.5
6612	Cement	87,353	156,787	1.03	1.21	39.7
8414	Clothing, accessories knit	28,836	65,525	0.34	0.50	63.6

Source: Data compiled from tapes of United Nations trade statistics.

nes = not elsewhere specified.

Note: SITC items 8617 and 8971, which appear on this table, are not shown in Table 1 because imports from Canada in 1987 were less than $20 million.

emphasize is that trade diversion to the detriment of Mexico is possible, and Mexico must take this into account in its future trade policy.[15]

The terminology, the reference to trade diversion, is misleading. If trade diversion occurs, it will affect more than Mexico's merchandise exports. Depending on the margin of preference for particular products and potential nontariff protectionism in the United States, U.S. firms will have incentives to choose Canada for new or expanded investment to supply the combined U.S.–Canada market.[16] These location choices could be at Mexico's expense.[17] It is important to keep in mind that because of the FTA, Canada will be more shielded from future U.S. nontariff measures than will Mexico. One reason that Canada decided to seek a free trade agreement with the United States was the expectation, or at least the hope, that such an agreement would lead to upgraded industrial technology necessary to supply the large combined market. Thus, if new industrial investment chooses Canada rather than Mexico, the ripple effect on Mexico would be a loss of newer technology.[18]

Industrial relations between Mexico and the United States have increasingly involved production sharing in the two countries by affiliated or related firms. Engines are produced in Mexico for use in U.S. automobiles; basic ingredients are made in the United States to produce pharmaceuticals in Mexico. Production sharing has been most extensive in the *maquiladora*—this is essentially what the *maquila* plants represent[19]—but is by no means limited to them. It is possible that the FTA will disrupt this growing trend of complementary production, and hence of trade, between Mexico and the United States in many industries.

MEXICO'S OPTIONS

A combined diversion—trade, investment, technology, production sharing—if it takes place, will be progressive as the margins of preference under the Canada–U.S. FTA come gradually into play over the next ten years, or as future U.S. nontariff protectionism affects imports from Mexico and not Canada. Intellectually, Mexico can now see the consequences of growing discrimination in its main market—its overwhelmingly most important market—but the effect will hit home only as and if it becomes reality. And this reality could change attitudes in Mexico about seeking an arrangement that protects it from the adverse consequences of the Canada–U.S. FTA. This could include not just sector agreements, but, over time, even reconsideration of a full-fledged free trade agreement with the United

States or entry into a NAFTA. This gradual process occurred in Western Europe as the community of six grew to the community of twelve that exists today.[20] The additional six countries saw things differently over time when faced with facts. I am suggesting that if the Canada–U.S. FTA works as intended, Mexico will also see things differently with the passage of time.

The most comprehensive long-term option for Mexico is evidently to join in a NAFTA or to seek a free trade agreement just with the United States.[21] A NAFTA might be more congenial than a bilateral agreement precisely because it would provide Mexico with a companion country—one with which Mexico has few emotional scars—in free trade relations with the United States.[22] However, for reasons already stated, particularly those related to its relative underdevelopment, Mexico is unlikely to make this decision in the short term.

The choice Mexico has made, even if in a somewhat inchoate fashion, is to suggest sector agreements with the United States. (Such agreements could be trilateral as well.) These suggestions predated the Canada–U.S. FTA, and the pressure to proceed along sectoral lines is likely to grow. A sectoral approach poses serious problems. The first is legal; free trade between two (or three) countries would violate the most-favored-nation provision of article I of the GATT without conforming to the "substantially all" provision of article XXIV, which sanctions free trade areas and customs unions. Hence, each sectoral agreement would require a GATT waiver or if many such agreements were put forward simultaneously, a combined waiver could cover them. It is far from clear that the contracting parties would grant such a waiver or waivers.[23]

Beyond the legalities, a bilateral (or trilateral) sector-by-sector approach requires that a balance of benefits and costs be found in each sector. The tendency would be for each country to propose free trade in sectors where it believes it has most to gain, and to shun those in which its costs would be greatest.[24] One way to get over this hurdle is to negotiate in several sectors at once to work out the balance. But this expedient would expose the trade-offs between sectors in a stark fashion. The politics of overtly imposing costs on one sector so that another sector in the country can benefit would be excruciatingly complex (in my view, "impossible" would be more accurate).

The value of a full-fledged free trade agreement is that the trade-offs among sectors are implicit. The trade-offs do not escape the notice of those industries that may be adversely affected, but these interests are more easily submerged in the generalized advantages that are seen to accrue from free trade. The complete free trade approach, despite its greater original complexity, is probably much simpler in negotiating and political terms than a sector-by-sector negotiating process.

My judgment is that the sectoral approach has limited promise for Mexico as an answer to the FTA. This does not mean that no sector could demonstrate a balance of benefits and costs—quite possibly the automotive industry could, perhaps even trilaterally—but rather that a sectoral approach is only a partial solution. It is not a complete Mexican response to the FTA.

To the extent that the Uruguay Round of trade negotiations is successful in reducing U.S. and Canadian trade barriers, it would reduce margins of tariff preference under the FTA. If Mexico can get the United States to bind a significant number of tariffs in the Uruguay Round, this would also provide modest assurance against future U.S. tariff increases. (I use the word "modest" because future U.S. protectionism is more likely to take nontariff than tariff form.) The FTA has introduced an element into the multilateral trade negotiations that did not exist before for Mexico: the need to identify, in greater detail than done in this essay, the precise commodities in which the potential for trade diversion is greatest. Doing so would enable Mexico to focus on these products in its Uruguay Round negotiations with the United States and Canada. Mexico, therefore, has a large stake in the Uruguay Round. Assuming that balance can be found in specific sectors, the sectoral and the Uruguay Round approaches need not be exclusive.[25]

Another option open to Mexico is to look toward one or more agreements with the United States that are less comprehensive than a free trade agreement, but at the same time more expansive in their coverage of trade-related issues, as opposed to trade issues per se. For example, the United States seeks modifications in Mexican policies on foreign investment, protection given to intellectual property, access by U.S. firms in the Mexican transportation market, openness to other U.S. service industries, and purchases of U.S. telecommunications equipment. Mexico, for its part, wishes better access to the U.S. transportation market (such as for trucking). It would like to be consulted in advance of new protectionist measures, especially nontariff barriers, being contemplated by the United States. The procedures for dispute settlement between the two countries could be strengthened.

This is an agenda for constant dialogue between Mexico and the United States on trade and trade-related issues. Where such discussion will lead over time depends on whether specific successes occur and on the evolution of the Mexican and U.S. economies.

This discussion has focused on the options open to Mexico to confront the challenge of the free trade agreement between Canada and the United States. These two countries, in turn, have an obligation to seek to limit the damage the FTA might inflict on Mexico. The statement is especially germane for the United States. If trade diversion does seem likely for particular products, the two countries may wish to consider including these in the Uruguay Round. This approach would generalize the trade liberalization for such products, which they may not desire. Alternatively, both Canada and the United States can place products for which the FTA would divert Mexico's trade on their generalized system of preference eligibility lists without extending these preferences to all countries.

None of the options discussed would have the overall impact of a Mexican free trade agreement with the United States or Mexican entry into a NAFTA. The options other than that of a free trade agreement are ameliorative rather than corrective. They do have the merit, however, of approaching issues in manageable bites without prejudice to Mexico's inclusion in such an agreement when the time is right. If the FTA causes substantial diversion of Mexico's trade, the pressure on Mexico to examine the free trade option will grow. Indeed, the pressure may in time become inexorable.[26]

CONCLUSIONS

The conclusions have already been signaled.

- Mexico is unlikely to see itself as part of the free trade movement in North America for the time being. This assertion is based on the economic differences between Mexico and the other two countries, Mexico's great concern about more economic dependence on the United States, and Mexico's deep-grained philosophic desire to be master (sovereign) in its own house.

- However, Mexico has already begun to position itself to participate more broadly in world trade. This has involved more extensive trading and economic relations with the United States than would have been contemplated a decade ago.

- Mexico has started to examine how it can protect itself against trade diversion that may result from the Canada–U.S. FTA. Suggestions about bilateral sector agreements with the United States are one form this is taking. Mexico has also upgraded its representation to the GATT in Geneva.

- Mexico has additional options, such as embarking on a process of concluding trade and trade-related agreements with the United States (and perhaps with Canada) to foster habits of negotiation and cooperation. This, indeed, is being done.

- Over time, as the effects of the Canada–U.S. FTA are more fully felt, and if they do prejudice Mexico's own trade expansion (as I believe they will), the pressure to join in a wider free trade arrangement in North America will grow.

NOTES

1. Antonio Salinas Chávez, "Aspectos de la apertura comercial," *Comercio Exterior* 37, no. 10 (1987), pp. 807–814.
2. Because the government owns the majority interest in all domestic banks, whether export credit from them is public or private is not clear. The

support of other institutions—for example, the Banco Nacional de Comercio Exterior—is clearly official. A financial structure parallel to the
nationalized banking system has also developed.
3. Banco Nacional de México, *Review of the Economic Situation of Mexico* 64, no.
752 (1988), pp. 307–308.
4. This was the emphasis of the remarkably successful presidential campaign
of Cuauhtémoc Cárdenas. He did not win the election on July 6, 1988, but
he was awarded 31 percent of the vote. Carlos Tello Macías, an economist
on the left wing of the Partido Revolucionario Institucional, has advocated
a "new internal economic order," which would not call for privatization of
public enterprises, but would raise their efficiency. See his "El estado y la
economía mixta," *Nexos* 11, no. 128 (1988), pp. 25–30.
5. At the most basic level, "success" means restoration of economic growth,
and this, in my judgment, will require more relief from the burden of
servicing the external debt than was accomplished in Mexico's agreement
with the commercial banks in 1989.
6. The report of the Bilateral Commission on the Future of United States–
Mexican Relations, *The Challenge of Interdependence: Mexico and the United
States* (Lanham, Md.: University Press of America, 1989), recommends
that the two countries "move promptly to free-trade agreements in all
sectors where benefits from free trade may exist, especially in industrial
sectors" (p. 67). This commission was composed of private persons from
both countries, but many of the key Mexicans had close ties with the
government and presumably would not have consented to this recommen-
dation without official consent.
7. The calculation is based on data from the Bank of Mexico.
8. The *maquiladora* are plants for which foreign inputs are imported in bond,
processed or further manufactured, and then, generally, exported. When
U.S. inputs are used and the *maquiladora* product is imported back into the
United States, the duty is paid only on the value added in Mexico. This has
been the fastest-growing portion of Mexico's exports; in 1987, it made up
25 percent of all exports of manufactures, as calculated on the basis of
value added in Mexico.
9. A limitation on payments of external debt is still possible if the negotiated
reduction in 1989 turns out to be inadequate.
10. Larry Rohter, "Mexico Opens Its Economy And The Imports Flood In,"
The New York Times, December 26, 1988, p. 41.
11. Ricardo Peñaloza Webb, "Elasticidad de la demanda de las exportaciones:
La experiencia mexicana," *Comercio Exterior* 38, no. 5 (1988), pp. 381–387,
concludes that the income elasticity of Mexico's nonpetroleum exports to
the United States is relatively high.
12. Recorded trade between Canada and Mexico is relatively low, but this
masks the inputs of each country embodied in products exported by the
United States to the other country.
13. President Salinas has publicly ruled out either option on at least two
occasions.
14. The United Nations tapes used to construct Table 1 are based on data
provided by the United States. Imports from *maquiladora* in Mexico thus
include both the inputs exported by the United States for processing in

bond in Mexico and the value added in Mexico. Many products listed in Table 1 come from *maquiladora*.

15. So must the United States and Canada if they do not wish the FTA to harm Mexico, but the initiative is most likely to come from the country with most at risk. While obtaining preferential tariff treatment may not have been an important motive for entering the FTA, Canadian producers now have a vested interest in these preferences in the U.S. market.

16. Similar incentives will emerge for Canadian investment in the United States to supply the combined market, but this is now less relevant for Mexico because its foreign investment comes predominantly from the United States.

17. There may also be an incentive to choose *maquiladora* over other investment in Mexico, to take advantage of the provisions of U.S. tariff items 806.30 and 807.00. For *maquiladora* products, the margin of preference will be applicable only for the value added in Mexico, and not for the total value of the U.S. import.

18. At the margin, Mexico could improve its attractiveness as a location for foreign direct investment by easing its legal restrictions on foreign equity proportions and reducing the red tape involved in getting approval for investment proposals. Steps on the latter were taken in May 1989.

19. This is the theme of Joseph Grunwald and Kenneth Flamm, *The Global Factory: Foreign Assembly in International Trade* (Washington, D.C.: Brookings Institution, 1985).

20. It is unlikely that twelve is the limit. Norway, which earlier rejected entry into the European Community, is now reconsidering that decision, and other countries have applied or are considering applying for entry.

21. Mexico might consider a free trade agreement with Canada as a way station to a NAFTA, but this is unlikely. In his inaugural address, Salinas specifically mentioned Canada as a country with which Mexico should intensify economic relations. Nevertheless, intensified trade relations need not involve an FTA consistent with article XXIV of the GATT.

22. Europe has parallels. The Netherlands, for example, has less trouble joining with West Germany in the European Community than it would have in a bilateral customs union.

23. During the debate that led up to the Canadian request for the FTA negotiations, there was the suggestion by a witness in hearings held by the Standing Senate Committee on Foreign Affairs of Canada that if enough sectors were included in sectoral agreements, this, combined with the U.S.–Canadian trade that was already free of tariffs, would permit the two countries to assert they were in conformity with GATT article XXIV. Similar suggestions have been made by Timothy Bennett, a former official of the Office of the U.S. Trade Representative, regarding U.S.–Mexican sectoral agreements. Little is new in the world.

24. This is precisely what happened when Canada suggested a sectoral free trade approach to the United States. The negotiations broke down. One Mexican observer commenting on this essay suggested that just as Canada had to go through the sectoral approach before it came to the FTA, Mexico must do the same.

25. The Uruguay Round approach, in my judgment, holds greater promise for Mexico than the sectoral approach.
26. My judgment is that Mexico will come to the conclusion that a bilateral free trade agreement with the United States is desirable before the United States does. Mexico is concerned about its unequal development. The U.S. concerns about an agreement with Mexico will focus on wage disparities, and a debate on this theme is apt to become highly emotional.

6

THE IMPLICATIONS FOR THE FUTURE OF U.S. TRADE POLICY

Peter Morici

The decision of the United States to conclude a comprehensive free trade agreement with Canada was a milestone in U.S. trade policy. However, a preferential agreement with its largest trading partner, along with a surge in interest in negotiating other bilateral arrangements and protectionist pressures in the United States, raises issues about the direction of U.S. policy. Certainly, the consequences of the Canada–U.S. Free Trade Agreement (FTA) for continued U.S. support of an open multilateral system should be considered; however, the FTA's implications for U.S. trade policy are much broader and often more subtle.

First, the FTA process has taught us several lessons about modern regional and multilateral trade negotiations—most notably, how difficult and complex they have become. With their greater emphasis on nontariff issues, these discussions touch increasingly on matters of domestic policy and culture that twenty or even ten years ago seemed firmly within the boundaries of national prerogatives. The nontariff issues the United States and Canada are addressing under the FTA tell us much about the constraints that will be imposed on their domestic policies as both countries seek greater liberalization through the General Agreement on Tariffs and Trade (GATT), and about how difficult true multilateral progress on some issues could prove to be.

Second, aside from some bilateral irritants and strictly regional issues, the core of U.S. objectives for the FTA is quite similar to the U.S. agenda for the Uruguay Round. The FTA negotiations illustrate, in areas such as subsidies, some of the parameters that may define what the United States can hope to achieve in multilateral negotiations, as well as the impediments to progress created by U.S. policies and approaches to negotiations.

Third, U.S. commitments to Canada under the FTA may constrain U.S. actions toward third countries. Several key questions emerge: Beyond the trade diversion associated with a free trade area or customs union, will the FTA engender discrimination against third countries? Does the FTA represent a U.S. step toward bilateralism and a weakened U.S. commitment to multilateralism and the GATT? Does it give added impetus to regionalism in the global trading system? How does the FTA increase the stake the United States and Canada each have in arrangements the other negotiates with third countries?

Fourth, broader issues relate to the future of the GATT system. This essay argues that the FTA does not signal a reduced U.S. commitment to multilateralism and that it is more an aspect of the trend toward regionalism than one of that trend's motivating forces. Yet, it is important to recognize that not all regional trade agreements are created equal. Some could contribute to, or at least be consistent with, long-term multilateral progress, while others could impede progress; and drawing distinctions is not always easy. Moreover, a proliferation of additional regional agreements could pose real dangers to the GATT system.

LESSONS ABOUT MODERN TRADE NEGOTIATIONS

By the conclusion of the Tokyo Round, it had become a cliché to say that tariffs were no longer the principal impediments to trade and that the primary focus of future trade negotiations must be nontariff barriers. Together, the FTA, the Australia–New Zealand Agreement, and the European Community (EC) 1992 process illuminate the limits and certain implications of this statement.

It is important to recognize that significant tariffs remain. The Tokyo Round cuts left in place high tariffs on textiles, apparel, and other basic manufactures for which the industrialized countries use a variety of tactics to restrain imports from newly industrializing countries (NICs) and other suppliers. Governments of industrialized countries have an incentive to focus on nontariff issues, in part because they believe their economies are already absorbing about all the NICs' products they can politically endure in many high-tariff industries.[1] Other significant tariff barriers remain among the industrialized countries. For example, at the beginning of the FTA negotiations, high tariffs were in place in one or both countries on furniture, appliances, cosmetics, and recreational boats, as well as on some petrochemicals, plastics, nonferrous metal products, paper products, and fish products. As the discussions began, trade policy analysts talked about the possibility of excluding some "sensitive sectors" and considered what share of bilateral trade would have to be duty-free to satisfy the requirements of GATT article XXIV.

The FTA, the Australia–New Zealand Agreement, and the EC experience make clear that all tariffs can be eliminated among nations at similar levels of economic development, including those in depressed or trade-sensitive sectors, like basic nonferrous metals and automotive products. However, the FTA's tough rules of origin for automotive products indicate that as tariffs are brought down on a regional basis, jointly implemented or common nontariff barriers toward third countries may evolve to maintain, or even increase, protection for politically potent, mature industries.[2] Although highly competitive exporters, such as those in Japan and particular NICs, may be the targets of such actions, these measures can adversely affect other industrial- and developing-country producers that pose no great threat to firms and workers within regional trading areas. Given the FTA's provisions for automotive products, the United States and Canada should not be surprised to see the EC implement "transitional" measures to replace national import regimes (in automobiles, for example) as part of its 1992 process, or to see new EC product standards that impose impediments to U.S. and Canadian sales in Europe.[3] Moreover, once jointly implemented protective structures are put in place as part of the political process of establishing or extending regional trading areas, they become particularly difficult to eliminate and can become progressively more discriminatory.[4]

The above-mentioned trade agreements also make plain that agreements establishing regional free trade areas, characterized by substantial mutual trade dependence and integration of production, must address nontariff measures, services, investment, and the application of trade remedy laws, if they are to be meaningful. The recent history of U.S.–Canadian trade relations provides clear examples of how practices in these areas can offset or limit the benefits anticipated from tariff reductions.

However, in addressing nontariff issues, U.S. and Canadian negotiators have taken on much greater problems than transparency and the absence of an "intent" to discriminate in areas like product standards and professional licensing. The freer movement of goods and services often requires greater compatibility or interface of domestic policies, practices, and regulations; these vary among countries in their rigor and structure, owing to differences in national values, as well as certain objective conditions (including levels of economic development and industrialization). Policy coordination raises important microeconomic policy issues. It can involve bridging differences in national ideologies concerning the appropriate roles for and methods of government in ensuring the safety, quality, and integrity of consumer goods and professional services; competitive pricing in the provision of services; and the soundness of financial institutions. Matters such as educational requirements for architects and accountants, the definition and protection of intellectual property, and the management of the banking system reach deeply into national policy prerogatives, and these can raise important issues related to sovereignty. In the end, policymakers can be faced with difficult trade-offs as they confront choices between ceding some power over particular levers of national economic or social policy and impeding a process of liberalization that could facilitate the freer flow of goods, improved competitiveness, and greater prosperity.

Moreover, not all barriers to trade result from overt government actions; many emanate from differences in national cultures and institutions that are beyond the control of governments. For example, consider the difficulties U.S. construction companies continue to encounter in Japan despite important Japanese government efforts to achieve improvements.

The FTA has created interest in U.S. or Canadian free trade agreements with Mexico and at least one of the Asian-Pacific nations. Solid economic and political reasons justify skepticism about the likelihood of other trade agreements similar to the FTA. The point here is that Japan, the East Asian NICs, and members of the Association of Southeast Asian Nations (ASEAN) have economic institutions, laws, and cultures that differ fundamentally from those of the United States and Canada, further diminishing the prospects for the intense micropolicy coordination necessary to ensure the scope and depth of progress the United States and Canada are committed to achieving in nontariff measures, services, and investment.[5] More likely options are framework agreements—similar to the U.S.–Mexico agreement—or a cooperative body—such as a Pacific version of the Organization for Economic Cooperation and Development (OECD).

The issues the United States and Canada are taking up in their continuing FTA discussions[6] are similar in scope to, even if not as ambitious as, the EC's 1992 agenda—such as product and technical standards, an open border for agricultural inputs and products, professional licensing, business services, investment, government procurement, and regulation (or deregulation) of financial markets. Also, the FTA agenda includes some issues for which the EC already has well-established procedures—a regional regime for subsidies, for example. The U.S.–Canada experience would seem to indicate that virtually unencumbered trade in goods and significant liberalization in services requires a level of consultation and domestic policy compatibility more closely identified with an economic community than with a free trade area. Indeed, it would appear that if the United States and Canada succeed in their efforts, they are creating an economic community without a common external trade barrier as much as they are forming a free trade area.[7]

The FTA process for nontariff barriers and services has major implications for multilateral trade negotiations. Owing to the institutional complexities discussed above, the agreement provides only a standstill on many nontariff and services issues— it establishes ambitious general requirements for *new* practices and commits the United States and Canada to long negotiating processes aimed at reducing existing barriers on a sector-by-sector and issue-by-issue basis. If the Uruguay Round is to achieve meaningful progress in these same areas, then codes of the kind negotiated in the Tokyo Round—no matter how well crafted and effectively complemented by an improved GATT dispute settlement mechanism—would only signal even more difficult and protracted negotiations. This raises questions as to whether it is ultimately possible or most efficient to try to achieve important objectives on some issues with all ninety-six members of the GATT participating at the same level. (See the discussion below on standards and services.)

LESSONS FOR U.S. TRADE POLICY

To appreciate what the FTA process may teach us about U.S. objectives and strategies in the trade negotiations, it is important first to recognize several of the broader forces affecting U.S. bilateral and multilateral relationships.

U.S. policymakers increasingly recognize the need to strengthen U.S. competitiveness through general policy initiatives such as improved education, tax reform, and incentives for research and development (R&D). However, the espoused thrust of U.S. industrial policy remains rooted in the view that for national economies to succeed, policymakers must generally accept international market signals, and governments should rely, as much as possible, on private decisions to allocate industrial resources.[8] A corollary to this basic notion is the U.S. belief that foreign government policies—for example, subsidies, special programs for emerging industries, and foreign investment regulations—intended to promote or sustain production in areas of traditional U.S. competitive strength—U.S. agriculture, technology-intensive products, and services—unfairly harm U.S. firms and workers and reduce global economic efficiency. The United States takes the position in trade negotiations that GATT participants should accept this basic approach to industrial policy by framing and accepting rules that limit significantly government prerogatives to influence international markets. This implies substantial disciplines on industrial and regional aids and other domestic policies.

Although the U.S. notion that national policies should be fundamentally responsive to international market signals has gained currency in recent years, espoused agnosticism in the United States about government intervention has not. Often, U.S. trading partners do not share the sense of urgency about the need to constrain domestic policies to ensure efficient allocation of resources and further open markets. Why? They frequently do not share U.S. perceptions about what constitutes market-responsive and market-oriented policies—specifically, they see governments as having important and effective roles to play in helping private firms decipher and respond adequately to market signals.[9]

The contrast between Japanese and U.S. performance on the competitiveness scoreboard gives American exhortations about the efficacy of nonintervention a certain credibility problem, as do increasing U.S. reliance on managed trade agreements in troubled sectors (for example, steel and semiconductors) and growing U.S. inclination to support emerging technologies on national security grounds.[10] Much the same may be said about U.S. concepts of what constitutes open markets, fair trade, and trade-distorting practices. The EC, while at best only doing about as well as the United States, sees the principal obstacles to its progress as intra-European and appears to give first (likely disproportionate) priority to internal reforms. In any case, 1992 reforms will reflect European perceptions about what is "open," "fair," and "distorting," as well as "digestible." This said, the United States has a tough row to hoe in negotiations on issues where its perceptions differ substantially from those of its trading partners (for example, subsidies); the United States is perceived to have more to gain (for example, services and agriculture); or harmonization or reform of domestic institutions with strong cultural underpinnings is critical (for example, standards and access to domestic distribution systems).

Where do Canada and the FTA fit in all this? Given the ideological tensions just discussed, two dimensions are worth considering. First, U.S. negotiators seem generally better able to achieve their objectives—either to open markets to U.S. exports or, hypocritically, to protect U.S. industries—when U.S. trading partners are most dependent on continued access to U.S. markets or capital. This is illustrated by recent concessions obtained from Korea on investment[11] and from Mexico on structural reforms, as well as by U.S. success with Japan on automobiles and, more widely, on steel.[12] Much the same may be said concerning Canada's about-face on the Foreign Investment Review Agency earlier this decade and, more recently, its willingness to deal on steel and softwood lumber. Such leverage is often, though not always, increased when the United States is negotiating bilaterally.[13] Although the dangers of U.S. reliance on bilateral leverage are apparent—specifically, it can serve myopic political interests as easily as it can serve the longer-term goal of liberalizing markets—it was clearly important during the FTA negotiations. Canada has the greatest stake in U.S. markets and was motivated by concerns about future U.S. protectionist actions.

Second, Canada's views about how government and business should interact are closer to those of the United States than are the views of other major trading partners. Therefore, it would seem that the FTA illustrates, on many issues, the important parameters defining what the United States may expect to achieve in broader international negotiations. In still other areas, the agreement illustrates what can and cannot be achieved in bilateral talks. Let us consider some issues.

Subsidies

The FTA subsidies negotiations indicate just how vexing this issue is for the United States and its trading partners. The United States would like to achieve greater discipline—in the simplest terms, to move away from reliance on countervailing duties after the fact by establishing some constraints on the use of subventions in the first place. This could be done through lists of prohibited and permissible actions, and rules to evaluate practices that are not on either list. For such a discipline to be a meaningful improvement over the present situation, it must not require an offended party to prove injury before countervailing when the offending party refuses to or cannot[14] remove the effects of the practice in question. This requirement raises at least four sets of problems, the first relating specifically to Canada, and the others relating more broadly to all U.S. trading partners:

- U.S. officials are reluctant to accept a blanket omission of regional development programs from a list of prohibited Canadian practices. Virtually all subsidies help both communities and industries, and Ottawa could easily provide substantial aid to an industry through regional agencies—it did so in the Michelin case. However, the United States has industrial and regional aids of its own, which Congress is unwilling to give up. This is especially problematic for negotiations with Canada, because the Congress may be particularly reluctant to accept a discipline on U.S. subsidies in exchange for a similar discipline on the actions of a country accounting for only one-fifth of U.S. trade—the "five-to-one problem."[15]

- Since the United States has done many of the same kinds of things as other industrial countries, but at lower levels of intensity (for example, the Economic Development Administration and industrial revenue bonds) or frequency (the Chrysler and Lockheed bailouts), and given the continuing issue of the competitive benefits bestowed by defense procurement on the U.S. computer, electronics, and aviation sectors, it would appear that the United States does not really want its trading partners to give up subsidies (then it would have to do the same). Rather, it seems the United States would like other countries to restrict themselves to a similar level and scope of activity, leaving the United States some room to maneuver.

- A key objective of U.S. trading partners during the Tokyo Round was to get the United States to accept an injury test for countervail. A subsidy discipline with border measures that do not require injury tests looks a lot like the old regime; such perceptions are important and would have to be addressed.

• Like it or not, the Canadians, Japanese, and Europeans see the potential interplay between competitiveness and structural adjustment policies, on the one hand, and subsidies, on the other, in a fundamentally different way than do U.S. negotiators, the administration, and many in Congress. To varying degrees, U.S. trading partners see more benefits or fewer costs in their governments' encouraging private responses to market opportunities to facilitate structural adaptation. This divergence of views, although by no means absolute, does inevitably lead to disagreements on a number of questions: When does government assistance cross the line and become unfair targeting? To what extent does aid to domestic firms in high-technology industries deny opportunities to foreign firms with hard-won, privately financed competitive advantages? Similarly, to what extent does aid to domestic producers in distressed industries shift adjustment burdens abroad?

Focusing on both U.S.–Canadian and multilateral negotiations, I am left with two observations on the subsidies issue. First, comprehensive solutions are not likely. I would not be surprised to see U.S.–Canadian and multilateral negotiators move toward a compromise approach of the kind Gary Horlick and Debra Steger suggest in chapter 4—one aimed more at containing the problem than at completely resolving it. In both bilateral and multilateral frameworks, a discipline prohibiting some of the most trade-distorting practices and other direct aids to firms above x percent of shipment or capital costs would give the United States the flexibility it requires to continue its industrial aids, while providing Canada and other trading partners with something in return for the industrial benefits created by U.S. defense expenditures. In the U.S.–Canadian context, such an approach could also provide the basis for compromise on regional aids and a solution to the five-to-one problem.

Second, a considerable amount, but by no means all, of the subsidy problems the United States encounters with its trading partners relate to adjustment issues, and while the United States may subsidize less, U.S. trading partners are quick to point out that it frequently uses other means to aid mature industries and promote emerging ones.[16] Often these have been reactive policies. For example, the U.S. government has generally been unwilling to structure comprehensive programs for distressed industries that could help firms and workers overcome barriers to adjustment. For the most part, it has considered assistance to mature industries only after their backs were to the wall, and then it has frequently yielded to political pressures for protectionist solutions (for example, voluntary restraint agreements in automobiles and steel), as opposed to relying principally on measures that promote positive adjustment. A great deal of the growth in the scope of protected U.S. industries has resulted from the private sector's refusal or inability to adjust, the federal government's political inability to make a gray-area measure degressive,[17] and its disinclination toward formulating positive adjustment policies.

At the end of the day, both in its discussions with Canada and in the GATT, the United States may have to temper its position on subsidies and the appropriate role for governments in fostering industrial change, and acknowledge a more proactive approach to policy. The provisions relating to adjustment programs and section 201 actions in the 1988 Trade Act represent some movement in this direction, but probably not very much. With respect to Canada and the FTA, negotiating a prohibition on the most trade-distorting subsidies and adopting an x percent rule for other direct aids would represent this sort of compromise; further joint approaches to adjustment in industries organized on a binational basis or characterized by cross-border rivalries, regardless of how ambitious that may seem, may prove to be an important way to reduce tensions over subsidies.[18]

Such a movement in U.S. policy may prove to be less difficult in practice than in ideology. The Defense Department's growing concerns about continued access to secure (that is U.S.) technology[19] and the administration's initiatives in semiconductors and high-definition television, as well as U.S. protectionist actions in a range of mature industries, belie American laissez-faire inclinations. Moreover, these trade and industrial policies do not indicate a clear desire to frame a more market-responsive, proactive approach to policy. For the Reagan administration, which campaigned on a platform to eliminate excessive government regulation and intervention in private decision-making, public recognition of a positive role for government in fostering industrial change was too difficult. The lack of clear industrial policy planning has resulted in a peculiar mixture of market-oriented domestic deregulation and ad hoc, sometimes market-responsive, sometimes protectionist industrial and trade policies. The Bush administration is proving to be less burdened by ideology on a broad range of issues and may be able to recognize that industrial policy planning (even if pursued under a more politically acceptable title) could be one means to achieve greater internal discipline on U.S. trade policy.

Standards and Services

FTA chapters covering standards and services indicate just how laborious these areas are. Even at the bilateral level, it was possible to take only some measures to assure transparency, reduce the obstacles posed by testing and certification, establish broad goals for the reduction of barriers, and begin a process of sector-by-sector discussions. This seems to indicate that the best way to bring down barriers in multilateral talks may be to accept, initially, similar broad agreements as adequate progress, and then try to work out difficulties among smaller groups of nations at comparable levels of economic development.

For example, in services, the industrialized and developing countries could be asked to agree on the kinds of general provisions contained in the FTA that apply to new laws and regulations. Meanwhile, the industrialized countries could decide to go further with sector-by-sector talks on an agreed upon schedule. The industrialized countries could leave the door open to the NICs and other developing countries to join in this process.

Foreign Investment

The United States achieved much of what it was seeking in the FTA with regard to foreign investment. These objectives include national treatment of U.S. subsidiaries once established in Canada and a ban on performance requirements directly affecting trade—in particular, requirements to export specific shares of production, substitute imports with domestic goods, or achieve goals for domestic content. However, Canada maintains the right to screen U.S. acquisitions of financial institutions and its largest industrial corporations.

It is significant that the FTA does not address efforts to obtain promises from multinational corporations to undertake R&D and grant world product mandates, and does not deal with other, similar technology-related issues. Canadian trade officials interpret this absence of restrictions on certain performance requirements as legitimizing them. The Congress does not share this view, and highly visible Canadian efforts to obtain such technology-related commitments as prominent instruments of industrial policy would likely attract strong reactions from Washington. However, U.S. efforts to negotiate restrictions on these practices (as mandated by the Congress in the FTA implementing legislation) will encounter the same kinds of problems as U.S. efforts to eliminate subsidies as tools of industrial and regional policy. Thus, the Canadian federal and provincial governments probably could choose to discuss undertakings with multinational corporations that are amenable to some concessions and unlikely to complain, and to seek product mandates and R&D projects on a limited, low-profile basis. For these reasons, the concession the United States obtained in the FTA for trade-related performance requirements may define for now the limits that other trading partners would likely be willing to accept or, at least, what the United States could effectively enforce.

Agriculture

Although the FTA achieved much on essentially North American issues—for example, market access for local crops and a program to achieve an open market through harmonization of standards—it left the difficult problem of major farm support programs for resolution in the Uruguay Round.[20] Bilateral negotiations cannot resolve problems in commodity markets that are fundamentally global in scope. For some issues, the potential for progress is much greater in multilateral talks than in bilateral discussions.

THIRD-COUNTRY RELATIONS

The FTA has important consequences for U.S. commercial relations with third countries. These emanate from the constraints imposed on U.S. policy toward third countries by some of the preferential treatment the United States is now committed to giving Canada; the potential contribution of the FTA to U.S. bilateralism and the undercurrent of regionalism present in the multilateral trading system; and the stake the United States and Canada have in each other's policies toward third countries.

Constraints on U.S. Policies Toward Third Countries

The United States is now formally committed to preferential treatment for Canada in ways that could also lead to discrimination against third countries—in particular, beyond the trade diversion usually associated with free trade areas. The most significant examples are the FTA's tough 50 percent content requirements for automotive products[21] and the special treatment that will be afforded Canada when the United States takes GATT article XIX actions.

As regards global safeguard actions, the United States may include imports from Canada only if they are determined to be a substantial source of injury, but the United States must permit these imports to grow at their trend rate.[22] While the preferential treatment is technically limited to safeguard actions, this principle could become the baseline for imports from Canada under further U.S. programs of voluntary restraint agreements (VRAs).[23] Should the United States further limit imports of resource-based manufactures, such as nonferrous metals during the next recession, special status for Canadian products would impose additional burdens on developing-country producers. Moreover, given the U.S. political stake in the success of export-oriented structural reforms now under way in Mexico, the United States may be constrained by self-interest to give Mexican exports similar treatment on a de facto basis. If a case emerges involving both Mexican and Canadian exports, then the outcome for other exporters could be very harsh.

It is important to recognize, though, that given the nature and scope of the FTA, the likely alternative to this approach would have been to give Canada a full exemption from U.S. global safeguard and similar gray-area actions—essentially the EC approach. This would have further increased the potential adverse effects of U.S. trade actions on third countries.

Also, the concessions the United States made to Canada on foreign investment screening and the automotive trade could prove to be of significant interest to Mexico.[24] Consider the former. The United States has agreed to exempt Canada from any foreign investment screening mechanism the United States might choose to put in place, even though, as noted above, Canada maintains the right to screen the acquisitions of financial institutions and its largest industrial corporations. Although the United States is in no way bound to give similar asymmetrical consideration to other partners in future free trade agreements, Mexico shares much with Canada in its dependence on U.S. capital, technology, and markets, and hence in its concerns about asymmetry in economic relations and sovereignty. Should economic reforms in Mexico reach the point of making some kind of U.S.–Mexican trade agreement possible, the FTA establishes a precedent for U.S. negotiators to consider an asymmetrical investment regime that embodies meaningful concessions from Mexico. Likewise, should a bilateral or trilateral agreement become feasible in automotive products, the FTA provides U.S. negotiators with a similar precedent to permit Mexico to continue some form of its performance requirements for foreign manufactures already established there in exchange for other concessions.

The FTA and the Drift Toward Bilateralism and Regionalism

Given the recent force of protectionist pressures in the United States and the growth in interest in negotiating other bilateral agreements, it seems appropriate to assess whether the FTA signals a weakened U.S. commitment to multilateralism and a continued U.S. drift toward bilateralism, thus providing additional impetus to the undercurrent of regionalism in the global trading system.

Whether or not the United States becomes more protectionist will not turn on its relationship with Canada, because protectionist pressures have their origins in forces that transcend U.S. relations with Canada, and unlike some other regional agreements, the FTA is broadly consistent with efforts to achieve multilateral progress both in the rules it establishes and in its effects on U.S. incentives.

Protectionist pressures in the United States emanate from competitive pressures on U.S. firms and workers. These, in turn, have their origins in misguided U.S. fiscal policies; lower net saving rates in the United States than in Japan and other countries; the inability of some businesses and workers to adjust adequately to shifting competitive conditions; and a general reluctance by the federal government to address these problems squarely.[25] Unimpeded Canadian access to the U.S. market will not significantly increase competitive pressures on U.S. firms and workers outside of some resource-based industries. Moreover, these are not industries of major concern to Japan, the EC, or many NICs.[26] Rather, the rationalization of production permitted by the FTA should strengthen the competitive position of North American firms vis-à-vis offshore competitors.

Bilateral and regional arrangements are not necessarily inconsistent with multilateral progress. Such arrangements weaken the GATT system when they are used to circumvent GATT disciplines or when they become substitutes for or impediments to broader, multilateral liberalization. U.S.–managed trade agreements in, for example, the automobile and steel industries certainly fall into the former category, but the FTA falls into neither. The FTA's provisions increase bilateral trade by extending the process of trade liberalization into many areas of the Uruguay Round agenda, and they do so in ways consistent with approaches currently under consideration in these discussions. The agreement's provisions are generally consistent with GATT disciplines.[27]

Canada accounts for only 20 percent of U.S. exports, and its market is already more open to U.S. products than are most other economies; therefore, the United States will potentially have as much to gain by extending the progress achieved under the FTA in areas such as standards, services, and investment in the GATT as it will gain under the FTA. Although it may be possible for the United States to achieve much progress in bilateral and plurilateral talks, agreements with third countries, comparable in scope and approach to the FTA, would be difficult—if not impossible—to negotiate. Efforts to improve U.S. market access outside the GATT serve U.S. economic interests only when they promote a more integrated and efficient North American economy in a manner consistent with GATT principles, while not diminishing prospects for further multilateral progress; the GATT is unable to address issues of importance to the United States; or the United States can anticipate or provoke progress in the GATT.

To say that the FTA, the EC 1992 program, and the Australia–New Zealand Agreement add impetus to the drift toward regionalism in the world trading community may be wrongheaded. These agreements are key components of this trend, not its sources. Among the motivating forces behind bilateral and regional agreements are (1) the increase in the number and range of development characteristics of participants in the GATT system, coupled with slower growth over the past two decades in the industrialized countries that established the GATT and remain its principal markets; and (2) the increased complexity and scope of issues on the GATT agenda. The first set of factors has magnified the adjustment costs and challenges national governments face as a consequence of new technologies, shifts in comparative advantages, international macroeconomic policy imbalances, and sovereign debt problems: maintaining political commitments to open markets and extending the scope of multilateral liberalization are clearly more difficult today than they were twenty years ago. With respect to the second set of factors, as discussed above, meaningful progress on many of the nontariff issues implies important adjustments in domestic policies, practices, and regulations—that is, difficult harmonization or increased compatibility of national regimes. These realities combine to make further meaningful multilateral liberalization, although still possible, economically painful, politically costly, and frustratingly slow.

In contrast, at the bilateral and regional level, adjustment costs resulting from trade liberalization are more predictable and hence more controllable; and the technical problems of harmonization coincident with addressing nontariff barriers, services, and investment issues are generally more manageable, because participants usually share much more in terms of economic, legal, and political institutions. Preferential arrangements are emerging and expanding, because they provide some of the economic benefits of broader multilateral liberalization but may entail fewer, more manageable costs for their participants and generally are easier and quicker to negotiate.[28]

This brings us to two sets of issues: the prospects for U.S. involvement in other regional or bilateral agreements, and the risks for the GATT system associated with a proliferation of preferential agreements.

Prospects for Other Bilateral or Regional Agreements

The FTA, like the EC 1992 program and the Australia–New Zealand Agreement, was attractive to political leaders because the anticipated balance of benefits and adjustment costs appeared to be predictable and favorable, and the FTA involves the interface of reasonably similar economic and legal institutions. When evaluating the prospects for other bilateral arrangements, similar in scope and approach to the FTA, it is instructive to ask to what extent these same conditions hold. All of the frequently suggested partners for the United States—Japan, the East Asian NICs, ASEAN, and Mexico—could impose substantially greater adjustment costs on the U.S. economy than Canada if given access to U.S. markets on terms comparable to those now being afforded Canada. Similarly, the interface of economic and legal institutions could prove much more difficult than should be the case for the United States and Canada. Uncertainties with respect to the latter could cause in one party or the other in an agreement to accept an unexpected imbalance of benefits and costs. This said, the most logical candidate for a major trade agreement with the United States is Mexico.

Considering labor, capital, and trade flows, the U.S. and Mexican economies are already substantially integrated. As in most bilateral commercial relationships, factor and trade flows obtain their primary impulse from differences in factor prices. In contrast to other NICs, the United States cannot significantly resist, constrain, or redirect the pressures created by industrialization and lower wages in Mexico through trade measures; in the long run, the United States must accept either Mexican goods, continued immigration pressures, or both. In turn, these pressures have secondary effects on Canadian market opportunities in the United States.

The economic pressures on the Mexican government to continue reforms will remain substantial. The success of these reforms requires ever-increasing access to U.S. markets for Mexican manufacturers, and, as the reforms continue, the proportion of Mexicans with a vested interest in outward-looking, export-oriented policies (as opposed to protectionist, import-substitution policies) grows. This makes more likely future Mexican acceptance of some internal changes that would increase the potential for interface between Mexican and U.S./Canadian economic and legal institutions. Similarly, as Mexico continues its reforms, the U.S. stake in Mexican progress is sufficient to justify accommodating U.S. responses to special Mexican economic and political requirements.

As was the case for the United States and Canada, the United States and Mexico have much stronger incentives for finding the political will to bridge their differences than for establishing relationships with countries outside North America. However, we should not overestimate the consequences of economic progress in Mexico and expect it to lead to full Mexican participation in the FTA any time soon. At least initially, many of the agreement's provisions would be simply too difficult for Mexico to accept fully—notably, the treatment of energy, investment, and export performance requirements.[29]

It is important to recognize that a Mexico–U.S. or Mexico–U.S./Canada agreement could cover tariffs and several of the key issues the FTA addresses without requiring concessions on both sides as rigorous as those in the FTA. Each side could begin with concessions consistent with its economic circumstances and political constraints; hence, such an agreement, while signaling real movement and liberalization on both sides, need not impose all the stress coincident with the breadth and depth of domestic policy harmonization the United States and Canada anticipate under the FTA. The United States and Canada embarked on their road to free trade with reciprocal tariff reductions in the 1930s, cooperation in defense production in the 1940s, successive rounds of GATT-sponsored tariff reductions, and the Automotive Agreement in 1965. Should economic reforms proceed fruitfully in Mexico, the United States and that country might consider a broader package, including the phased elimination of tariffs, a safeguard provision similar to the FTA mechanism for global actions, provisions liberalizing investment flows (though not to the extent achieved with Canada), and perhaps discussions on product standards.

Canada would have an important stake in whatever duty free trade arrangements the United States might negotiate with Mexico. By comparing U.S. bilateral trade with Mexican and Canadian trade, Sidney Weintraub finds the potential for diversion of U.S. imports from Mexico to Canada under the FTA in automotive products, petrochemicals, metals, paper products, textiles and apparel, some consumer durables, and machinery.[30] Mexico–U.S. agreements could reverse these effects. Moreover, further integration of Mexico's inexpensive wage base into the cost structures of U.S. firms could reduce Canadian competitiveness in the U.S. market. To only a limited degree would the FTA's rules of origins deflect U.S./Mexican products (that is, U.S. products with Mexican components) from the Canadian market.[31] Since the FTA does not establish a common external trade policy, neither country is strictly required to consider the effects of third-country agreements on its partner in the agreement. However, should the United States enter into serious negotiations with Mexico, common sense would require consultations: the FTA is an evolving instrument, and Canadian perceptions about the fulfillment of anticipated benefits will influence Canada's posture and responses to U.S. concerns in ongoing FTA negotiations.

Canadians could come to recognize that they would have significant interests at stake in an emerging Mexico–U.S. agreement, and they could seek a substantive role in the negotiations. By participating in whatever arrangements the United States and Mexico might negotiate, Canada could seek increased market opportunities to balance the effects of partial loss of its preferred status in the U.S. market and capture for its manufacturers most of the advantages obtained by U.S. firms by further accessing Mexican labor and other resources. More broadly, such considerations illustrate Canada's substantial stake in other bilateral arrangements that the United States might consider.

BILATERAL AND REGIONAL AGREEMENTS AND THE GATT SYSTEM

As stressed above, bilateral and regional agreements have become more attractive to policymakers, because they may provide some of the benefits that could be obtained through multilateral liberalization with fewer, more manageable adjustment costs, and they are easier to negotiate. However, if we begin with the operating premise that multilateral liberalization best promotes economic efficiency and is our ultimate goal, then we should be concerned about how the emergence of new preferential agreements and expansion of existing ones affect the prospects for multilateral progress. It seems appropriate to ask several questions when new agreements are proposed or existing ones are extended.

First, beyond the inevitable trade diversion associated with simply removing existing trade barriers among members, do these agreements raise new barriers to commerce with nonmembers? No agreement is likely to be completely clean in this regard—consider the FTA's automobile rules of origin. However, aberrations should be kept to a minimum, and they should be justified in terms of offsetting concessions to and broader gains for nonmember countries (the latter include dynamic growth effects in member economies that create increased market opportunities for members and nonmembers alike).

The second question focuses on the more controlled benefits and adjustment costs associated with bilateral and regional, as opposed to multilateral, agreements: Do the agreements foster stronger economies, with increased capacities for accepting the adjustments associated with broader, multilateral liberalization?

Third, do they approach nontariff issues in ways that are consistent with past or potential progress on the same issues in the GATT? For example, in making national standards more compatible, liberalizing services, or addressing investment issues, are the rules and procedures to be established consistent with GATT principles? Are they at least as amenable as existing national practices to blending in with approaches under consideration or likely to evolve in the GATT?

Fourth, do the concessions member-countries make to each other preclude broader liberalization under the GATT, because the latter would upset the balance of benefits and costs in a politically unacceptable way? Does the regional arrangement create disincentives for participation in multilateral liberalization?

Generally, the FTA stands up well to these tests. The automobile rules notwithstanding, the agreement does not increase protection vis-à-vis third countries, its provisions are broadly consistent with GATT disciplines, and its agenda for liberalization and continued negotiations complements the Uruguay Round in its objectives and approaches. This is reflected in the positive response the FTA has received from trade officials abroad. The agreement should significantly strengthen the competitiveness of the Canadian and U.S. economies, improving their capacity to accept adjustments coincident with future multilateral liberalization. As discussed above, it does not create disincentives or obstacles[32] for the United States in seeking broader liberalization under the GATT. Multilateral progress continues to be an important goal for Canada as a means both for further broadening market opportunities and for balancing its growing commercial cooperation with the United States with expanded economic interests abroad.

The jury is still out on EC 1992. A more fully integrated European market will strengthen competitiveness and provide the potential for the EC to become more outward-looking. However, the additional industrial and institutional adjustments required by the sweeping scope of the 1992 program could sap for many years the EC's political and economic capacities to accept the further adjustments that could be imposed by a successful Uruguay Round or subsequent multilateral discussions.[33] Moreover, third-country governments and their private sectors have expressed considerable uncertainty and concern about the consequences of many 1992 initiatives for non-member-states. Among the key issues are the replacement of individual country import regimes with unified import rules in products such as automobiles and consumer electronics, the impacts of harmonized product standards and certification procedures on non-member market access, and the precise meaning of the term "reciprocity" as it relates to financial and business services.[34] How Europeans handle these issues will greatly affect whether the 1992 process substantially increases barriers to commerce with the United States, Canada, and other countries, as well as whether it facilitates or impedes multilateral progress.

A Mexico–U.S. or a Mexico–U.S./Canada agreement or process structured to be consistent with the FTA, even though less rigorous and ambitious, could stand up fairly well, but it would involve some risks. Like the FTA, such an agreement could be fashioned to be broadly consistent with GATT disciplines and complementary in its approaches to ongoing GATT discussions. It need not increase protection against offshore competition. It could strengthen the competitiveness of Mexico's economy, and Mexico's capacity to participate more fully in the GATT. In the *long run*, Mexico's fuller integration into the U.S. economy could prove to be a dynamic force for positive change and growth in the United States, and it would not create disincentives for the United States to seek progress in multilateral negotiations on most issues.[35] However, the latter becomes complicated for the United States if we focus on just mature industries. As noted above, the United States cannot significantly resist or redirect the adjustment pressures created by lower wages in Mexico. In the *short run*, though, would duty-free trade with Mexico increase the competitive pressures on mature industries enough to cause the United States to slow the growth of imports from other NICs and developing countries? While the specific provisions of an agreement with Mexico might not indicate an immediate increase in trade restrictions on imports from third countries, these could materialize through the U.S. safeguard and gray-area actions (providing preferential treatment to Canada and Mexico) and the application of other U.S. trade laws.[36] Should an agreement with Mexico tax the U.S. capacity to accept adjustments in mature industries, it would limit U.S. ability to make concessions to the NICs and developing countries in multilateral discussions and reduce U.S. prospects for winning concessions on matters such as services, intellectual property rights, and trade-related investment performance requirements.[37]

This brings to the foreground the very real problems of negotiating a succession of bilateral agreements after Israel, Canada, and Mexico. Consider the recontracting problem. The conclusion of future bilateral agreements could significantly reduce the preferences afforded and expectations engendered by earlier agreements.[38] As noted above, although the FTA does not give Canada proprietary rights to preferential treatment in the U.S. market, common sense requires that Canada's concerns be considered in discussions with Mexico or any other country; the same would apply to Mexico in discussions with still other countries should a Mexico–U.S. or Mexico–U.S./Canada agreement emerge. The consultations and renegotiations of existing agreements that could emerge each time another bilateral arrangement was proposed could become overwhelming, easily negating the advantages of bilateral and regional approaches. Much the same logic would apply to most bilateral agreements Canada would consider.

All of this would be messy enough if only tariffs were on the table; matters would get even more problematic with nontariff issues under discussion as well. Approaches to nontariff measures in a succession of U.S. bilateral agreements could vary with trading partners' business and legal traditions, cultures, and existing points of friction in bilateral trade. Individually, these agreements could be consistent with existing GATT rules; as a group, they could engender conflicting approaches to extending multilateral rules in areas such as services, intellectual property rights, and product standards. This problem would be exacerbated if a succession of U.S. bilateral arrangements were to be accompanied by a similar expansion of EC and Japanese arrangements with developing countries; arrangements centered on the United States, the EC, and Japan would almost certainly vary in their approaches to some issues and could be flatly inconsistent. It may not be possible to build up a workable set of multilateral rules on the basis of a succession of bilateral and regional agreements.

A U.S./Canada agreement with Mexico that envisions Mexico's increasing participation in the FTA could avoid this pitfall.[39] However, a series of individual bilateral agreements between the United States, Canada, or both, and Asian and Latin American countries could easily become counterproductive, creating obstacles to further multilateral progress. Similarly, U.S. or Canadian participation in a series of bilateral arrangements could limit further U.S.–Canadian progress envisioned through negotiations under the FTA. All of this argues for close U.S. and Canadian cooperation, and for both countries to proceed cautiously.

This should not preclude exploration of other institutional efforts to build cooperation or resolve frictions, however. Framework agreements, similar to the Mexico–U.S. agreement, and a Pacific version of the Organization for Economic Cooperation and Development deserve consideration.

CONCLUSION

The FTA process has broad implications for U.S. trade policy. It illustrates the difficulties inherent in modern trade negotiations—the challenges of bridging differences in economic and legal institutions, culture, and national interests to achieve progress on many nontariff, service, and investment issues. These indicate some of the parameters defining prospects for tangible progress in the Uruguay Round on subsidies, product standards, services, investment, and other areas. The FTA process also draws attention to the constraints imposed by genuine differences of views between the United States and its major trading partners concerning what constitutes market-responsive industrial policies, as opposed to unfair intervention in the workings of international commerce.

The FTA does not signal a weakened U.S. commitment to the multilateral system, nor does it represent an accommodation to protectionist pressures. Its provisions are broadly consistent with GATT disciplines, and the FTA agenda is complementary to the Uruguay Round in both its objectives and its approaches. As always, there are exceptions—most notably, the FTA's tough rules of origin for automotive products. Like North American and Asian concerns about EC 1992, the agreement illustrates that regional initiatives, while generally consistent with the GATT, may increase nontariff protection against third countries in selected industries.

The FTA may affect U.S. actions toward third countries. In particular, Canada's new privileged position under U.S. global safeguard actions may result in more restrictive measures directed toward third countries. Also, this provision, along with the differential treatment afforded Canada on foreign investment rules and Canadian automotive safeguards, could serve as a precedent for U.S. negotiators in seeking a balance of concessions in future agreements with other countries—particularly Mexico.

As for the prospects for other regional and bilateral agreements, it is important to recognize that political leaders have found such preferential arrangements attractive, because they perceive the balance of economic benefits and adjustment costs to be positive, predictable, and controllable, and the technical problems of policy harmonization coincident with nontariff issues manageable. In this regard, the FTA's ambitious scope and depth is made possible in part by the similarity of U.S. and Canadian economic and legal institutions. Other suggested U.S. partners in a regional or bilateral agreement do not have as much in common with the United States as Canada, making arrangements with them comparable in scope to the FTA less likely. This said, the U.S. and Mexican economies are already substantially integrated, and the United States and Mexico have much stronger incentives to find ways to bridge these kinds of differences than they have to develop relationships with countries outside of North America.

Additional regional or bilateral agreements would serve U.S. interests only if they promoted a more integrated and competitive North American economy while not diminishing prospects for multilateral progress, addressed issues the GATT is not ready to resolve, or anticipated or provoked progress in the GATT. Seeking ways to further liberalize trade with Mexico in a manner consistent with the FTA could meet these tests and yield important benefits to the United States, but certain risks are involved, and the United States should move cautiously. Canada would have an important stake in these discussions. Looking beyond Mexico, a succession of bilateral agreements could prove cumbersome and dangerous, reducing—as opposed to enhancing—prospects for multilateral progress. Therefore, although the FTA offers the United States and Canada important opportunities to liberalize bilateral commerce more rapidly than is possible under the GATT, the two countries should continue to place primary emphasis on the GATT in seeking progress with other trading partners. The GATT provides the most appropriate vehicle for liberalizing trade and opening markets outside North America.

NOTES

1. Eliminating many of these tariffs on a most-favored-nation basis would probably not affect the amount of protection these sectors receive. However, it would likely shift welfare effects of various quantitative restrictions (for example, in the United States, the Multifibre Agreement for textiles and apparel, and voluntary restraint agreements for automobiles and steel) more in favor of exporting countries. Specifically, the tariff revenues would be transferred from the importing-country government to those who obtain the rents from rationing the right to export to the industrial country. With voluntary restraint and orderly marketing agreements, these rents generally accrue to the exporting-country industries. Consider, for example, the premium prices paid for Japanese cars before the drop in the dollar, and beneficiaries of premium prices for some imported steel products during periods of tight supply.
2. The rules of origin require that to qualify for duty-free treatment, materials and components imported from third countries be incorporated into other goods or transformed in physically or commercially significant ways. In most cases, this requirement is met if a production process results in a

change in tariff classification or, as a backup requirement, if it results in 50 percent U.S./Canadian value added.

    The 50 percent rule is mandatory for automotive products. Moreover, this requirement is tougher than the 50 percent rule the United States applied under the Automotive Agreement of 1965. Unlike the old rule, it will not count overhead and indirect costs, thus increasing the protection afforded North American parts producers from offshore imports.

3. For example, "North American paper makers are particularly suspicious about new European health and safety standards, grades and testing procedures now being formulated." See "Paper Makers Fear New EC Barriers in 1992," *The Globe and Mail*, February 1, 1989, p. B-10.1.

4. Consider the EC Common Agricultural Policy, and now the Congress would like the FTA's rules-of-origin content requirement for automotive products raised from 50 percent to 60 percent.

5. Much the same may be said about Mexico, and to this must be added Mexican concerns about sovereignty and not becoming too economically dependent on the United States. However, as noted later in this chapter, the success of economic reforms in Mexico is critically dependent on increasing access to U.S. markets for Mexican manufactures, which may improve the climate for greater interface between Mexican and U.S./Canadian economic institutions.

6. For example, with respect to product standards, the United States and Canada are seeking greater compatibility and common certification procedures, even though the rigors of particular standards may be higher in one country than in the other. The EC is seeking more closely harmonized standards—for example, common specifications and floors.

7. This is not surprising. Prior to the FTA, the U.S.–Canadian commercial relationship had some important features of an economic community that had not yet been achieved in the EC. For example, Canadian restrictions on U.S. financial institutions notwithstanding, Canada and the United States already had a highly integrated capital market, something the EC is still seeking to complete; the two countries had policy coordination in the automotive sector and probably a better record on government procurement than the EC.

8. This is not to say that the U.S. government has not aggressively and significantly intervened in markets. Safeguard, gray-area measures, and the excessive use of unfair trade remedy laws are important examples; they represent reactive steps often taken to assuage politically powerful interest groups. The U.S. government provides aid to industry in other ways, notably in R&D–intensive activities through defense expenditures; however, in most cases, federal policymakers are not inclined to acknowledge their competitive benefits, or these policies are justified on national security grounds, perhaps with additional rationalizations flowing from government aid to civilian competitors in Japan and the EC.

9. An important distinction exists between "market signals" and "appropriate responses." Over the last decade, the American notion that governments should not and ultimately cannot resist international market signals on an economywide basis has gained currency. Mitterrand's failure to reassert France's sovereignty over its domestic market earlier in this decade proba-

bly has buried in Europe the idea that nations can *broadly* resist the forces of comparative advantages without incurring great costs. Although Europe seems willing to continue bearing such costs in agriculture, an important impulse behind the EC 1992 is to remove the protection afforded many national producers by member-states, at least as it relates to the intra-EC competition—that is, the internal market.

However, it is quite another thing to say governments do not have a broad role to play in ensuring that the private sector fully (or even adequately) responds to market signals. Indeed, European governments remain prepared to encourage and finance investments in technologies where they see a longer-term potential for self-sustaining competitive production. The notion that a valid and welfare-improving set of industrial policies is not achievable (at least in a practical sense, because policymakers are subject to political pressures) is a more isolated U.S. concept. This notion receives strong support among major players only from Canada and Britain; their support owes more, I suspect, to the predilections of their current governments than to sustainable trends in their political cultures.

10. For example, the Defense and Energy departments have recently identified twenty-two technologies, ranging from gallium arsenide to computer modeling to biotechnology materials and processing, as critical to national security. The two federal departments will now frame proposals for Congress to help finance these technologies. See Martin Tolchin, "Crucial Technologies: 22 Make the U.S. List," *The New York Times*, March 17, 1989, pp. D-1,3.
11. See John Boatman, "How Korea Stayed Off the Super 301 List," *Business International*, June 5, 1989, p. 170.
12. Conversely, U.S. frustrations in negotiations to obtain greater access to Japanese markets for semiconductors and agricultural products may reflect the absence of such leverage in those sectors.
13. Indeed, Canadian policymakers have long advocated the GATT as a forum in which Canada could create alliances with other participants in the trading system when negotiating on critical issues with major players such as the United States and the EC.
14. For example, in the case of capital subsidies.
15. See chapter 4, p. 95.
16. See, for example, Michael Hart, "The Future on the Table," presented at the Canadian Centre for Trade Policy and Law, University of Ottawa, Ottawa, Ontario, May 5, 1989.
17. Consider, in particular, textiles, steel, and automobiles.
18. See chapter 7, p. 163–166.
19. See note 10.
20. The FTA did establish the principle that each country will accept the other's grain exports when the exporting country's subsidies are less than or equal to the importing country's subsidies. For example, Canada will remove import restriction on U.S. wheat, oats, and barley when U.S. support levels are lowered to Canadian levels. Probably as significant, the FTA requires both countries to consult and take into account each other's export interests in offering export subsidies in third-country markets.
21. See note 2.

22. See chapter 1, p. 17.
23. With regard to VRAs, chapter 11 of the FTA may require some clarification. David Richardson notes that since chapter 11 does not specifically mention VRAs, U.S. officials could argue that it does not apply to them. Should chapter 11 fail to provide Canada with the same treatment under U.S. programs of VRAs as it does under U.S. safeguard actions, Canadians would view themselves denied important benefits anticipated from the FTA. See chapter 3, pp. 68–70.
24. Manufacturers of passenger vehicles and trucks that qualified for Auto Pact status prior to the FTA may continue to import passenger vehicles and trucks into Canada from third countries duty-free if they continue to assemble one car in Canada for each car sold there and achieve Canadian value added equal to 60 percent of Canadian sales. Among major suppliers of passenger vehicles, only General Motors, Ford, Chrysler, and Volvo so qualify.
25. As noted above, this is not to say the United States has not assisted distressed industries; rather, such efforts have often been protectionist, as opposed to promoting positive adjustment.
26. As indicated below, Mexico could prove to be a notable exception in metals.
27. An important exception is the provisions for automobiles. The situation with respect to safeguards is more difficult to evaluate. As noted above, the alternative to the FTA's global safeguard provisions would have been to exempt Canada completely from U.S. actions. However, U.S. acceptance of more Canadian imports in industries subject to import restraints would place even greater burdens on other U.S. trading partners.
28. The latter might not seem intuitively obvious, given the difficulties encountered, and the issues that remain, in the FTA and EC 1992 discussions. However, one must consider the amount of time that will ultimately prove necessary to achieve a truly similar breadth and depth of progress among all GATT signatories.
29. See chapter 5, pp. 110–111.
30. Ibid., p. 108n9.
31. Outside of textiles and automotive products, which are protected by stricter rules, the FTA's basic rule that components be incorporated into other goods or be transformed in ways that are physically or commercially significant would not likely pose a major barrier to exports of U.S./Mexican products into Canada.
32. While the FTA increases the stake that the United States and Canada have in each other's trade policy decisions, neither country has expressed a proprietary claim to preferential access to the other's market.
33. In northern EC countries, these adjustment pressures could be exacerbated by the continued assimilation of recent EC entrants Spain, Greece, and Portugal, and continued by dynamic growth in Italy.
34. C. Michael Aho and Sylvia Ostry, "Regional Trading Blocs: Pragmatic or Problematic Policy?," in William E. Brock and Robert D. Hormats, eds., *The Global Economy: America's Role in the Decade Ahead* (New York: The American Assembly, 1990), p. 157.
35. A free trade agreement with Mexico would not diminish incentives for the United States to engage Asian and European countries on issues such as services, intellectual property rights, and agriculture.

36. Theoretically, the FTA global safeguard provisions, which provide preferential access for Canada, pose the same dangers. However, the potential for Canadian disruption of U.S. markets in mature industries, other than nonferrous metals, is limited.

37. Much of what is said in this paragraph about the United States would apply equally well to Canada if the latter were to become a partner in a U.S. agreement with Mexico.

38. For a discussion of the recontracting problem, see Aho and Ostry, "Regional Trading Blocs."

39. The same might be true of a Mexico–U.S. agreement that envisions an evolution toward rules very similar to those of the FTA—the double FTA option.

7

LIVING WITH FREE TRADE

Peter Morici

The Canada–U.S. Free Trade Agreement (FTA) makes a good start toward establishing fully integrated markets for goods, services, and capital. Phasing out tariffs, most import and export measures, and duty drawbacks and remissions, the FTA ensures that most of the benefits of duty-free trade in goods will be achieved. Enshrining recently liberalized frameworks for direct investment and trade in financial services, it offers the potential for truly integrated capital markets. However, with regard to many nontariff barriers to trade in goods and business services, many benefits are prospective—in most cases, the FTA imposes a standstill on new discriminatory practices and establishes ambitious negotiating objectives for existing measures. Should these negotiations prove successful, the agreement would create an economic community in North America, less a common external trade policy, as much as it establishes a free trade area.

It is important to recognize that on the basis of commitments and compromises already achieved, Canada and the United States have made significant progress. Canada has enhanced its access to the U.S. market, and the global safeguard provisions have the potential to make this access more secure. The temporary dispute settlement mechanism for subsidies and dumping should build confidence that U.S. laws are administered objectively; however, the negotiation of a bilateral mechanism for subsidies remains an important Canadian goal. Canada maintains considerable freedom to support cultural industries and screen acquisitions of its largest industrial companies.

The United States can also claim important progress in the elimination of higher Canadian tariffs, improved market access for its highly competitive financial institutions, and comprehensive agreements for direct investment and business services, as well as the resolution of several narrower issues.[1]

This said, consider three observations. First, the FTA will achieve its full potential only if the U.S. and Canadian governments muster the necessary bureaucratic resources to implement effectively the commitments made under the agreement, and only if they find the political courage to accept the disciplines it establishes and carry its ambitious negotiating agenda through to meaningful conclusions.

Second, even as it currently stands, the FTA will fundamentally alter the conduct, substance, and style of bilateral relations. The agreement is now the primary mechanism for the management of the bilateral relationship, and its success will be central to Canadian perceptions about the United States and bilateral interactions. In Canada: "the FTA is seen as much more than a trade agreement—it marks a new relationship with the United States, and it therefore has a bearing on all bilateral issues, whether economic or not."[2]

Third, although the FTA's most significant consequences will be bilateral, U.S. motivations for negotiating it had a strong multilateral impulse, and the FTA has important implications for the conduct of U.S. and Canadian policies toward third countries.

Three sets of realities will strongly influence the consequent challenges that emerge for politicians and bureaucrats living with free trade: global economic pressures and continental adjustments; the general, unfinished, and evolving nature of the FTA; and the continuing evolution of the broader GATT system, of which the FTA (like other regional agreements) is now an important component. In many ways, how well the U.S. and Canadian governments stand up to these challenges, while coping with their commitments under the FTA, will signal how successful each will be in facing the broader challenges of the 1990s and the twenty-first century.

GLOBAL COMPETITIVE PRESSURES, ADJUSTMENTS, AND THE FTA

The United States and Canada face profound industrial adjustments, as the bases of their comparative advantages continue to evolve and technological developments fundamentally change the nature, scope, and structure of the competition and market opportunities industrialized countries face. Although bilateral liberalization will strengthen the North American economy in the long run, it will add to adjustment pressures in the short run, and these added pressures will create new bilateral issues. The initial issues that emerge should teach us much about the effectiveness of the FTA's institutional provisions—particularly the Canada–United States Trade Commission and the dispute settlement provisions—and provide guidance about modifications in the text of the agreement that may be needed. However, should the North American economy encounter a serious recession or some other event that sharply curtails market opportunities for U.S. or Canadian producers, the basic durability of the FTA could be subject to more rigorous testing.

U.S. Adjustment Issues and the FTA

For the United States, agriculture, high-technology, and service exports will remain important, but new foreign competitors mean greater emphasis on mature industries—for example, textiles, footwear, and automobiles. Not all mature industries will fare equally well.

The decline in the dollar from 1985 to 1988 helped improve sales and profitability in many mature industries. However, the long-term growth prospects of most basic metals industries in the United States are limited, raising quite distinct issues for nonferrous metals and steel.

David Richardson's summary of estimates indicates that the U.S. basic nonferrous metals industry could face a substantial employment loss as a result of free trade.[3] During the next recession, the superior competitive position of many Canadian producers, coupled with reduced or eliminated tariffs, could increase pressures on states with communities dependent on this industry to provide more competitive industrial incentives for attracting new employers or keeping old ones in business. Equally important, it could cause U.S. producers to run for cover under either the FTA's bilateral safeguard provisions or the broader remedies that may be obtained from U.S. trade laws.

The former would exacerbate the already unfortunate effects of competitive subsidization among states and provinces, while the latter would test the FTA's capacity to secure Canadian producers' access to the U.S. markets by insulating them from U.S. safeguard and gray-area trade actions, and the inappropriate use of U.S. dumping and subsidy countervailing duty laws.

With regard to steel, informal Canadian participation in the U.S. system of voluntary restraint agreements (VRAs) is contrary to the spirit of the FTA. While U.S. steel VRAs are almost certain to continue, integrated Canadian producers should be gradually disengaged from their discipline and permitted to participate more fully in the U.S. market.

The FTA provides Canada with some cover should U.S. industries obtain global safeguard protection—imports from Canada may not be reduced "below the trend of imports over a reasonable base period with allowance for growth" (article 1102). Should U.S. industries seek and receive protection from a program of VRAs, Canadian officials believe, this provision establishes the basis for avoiding a repetition of the steel episode. U.S. officials might argue that FTA article 1102 does not explicitly cover VRAs.[4] This issue needs to be clarified.

More broadly, if persistence of the U.S. trade deficit results in an avalanche of U.S. protectionism, then Canada's preferred status established by the FTA would be put to the test. Likewise, if the United States finally addresses its trade problems by reining in its budget deficit and reducing its appetite for foreign capital, then Canada, and other major U.S. trading partners, would face an additional source of industrial and labor market adjustments.

Canadian Adjustment Issues and the FTA

As discussed in chapter 1, growth opportunities for most of Canada's natural resource exports are limited. Free trade is hastening the rationalization of Canada's secondary manufacturing sector; this process is necessary for manufacturing to become more competitive and play a greater role in assuring growth and prosperity in the wider Canadian economy. However, in the short run, hastened industrial rationalization means greater labor force adjustments. The results Richardson presents indicate that the FTA will have little impact on overall Canadian manufacturing employment.[5] These results are generally consistent with the findings of industry studies undertaken for the Macdonald Royal Commission and the econometric forecasts of the Economic Council of Canada indicating that textiles, clothing, household furniture, and nonelectrical and electrical machinery and equipment face adjustments. Similarly, these results are generally consistent with the Economic Council's findings that metal fabrication and nonmetallic mineral products also face losses in employment shares.[6] It is important to recognize that while these industries may lose employment shares, absolute numbers of jobs may not decline greatly or at all. Normal growth and employee turnover should be enough to accommodate most interindustry adjustments; however, they do come on top of pressures for rationalization created by increasing global competition. A recession coupled with a substantial reduction in the U.S. trade deficit could give more poignancy to these adjustments and provide Canadian opponents of free trade with an opportunity to blame the FTA for hardships and problems having many other, more basic sources.[7]

So far, the Canadian government appears determined to deal with labor adjustments through greater emphasis on worker retraining. However, the confluence of ever-increasing global competitive pressures, the adjustments imposed by bilateral tariff reductions, a recession, and perhaps a reduction in the U.S. trade deficit could pose a real challenge to Canada's strategy—by increasing pressure on Ottawa to protect domestic industries through safeguard actions, subsidies, and procurement, or by adding more fuel to state-provincial competition for industry.

All of this points to the need for Canada's government to take every opportunity to inform the Canadian public about the ultimate sources and nature of the adjustments being imposed on their economy and to give real effect to the recommendations of the de Grandpre report by substantially increasing Canada's emphasis on worker training.[8] Further, the United States and

Canada must proceed promptly to address the subsidies issue and other negotiations pledged under the FTA and to quickly modify and correct shortcomings in the agreement as they become apparent. For example, if the safeguard provision fails to insulate Canada adequately from U.S. gray-area trade actions, then the two governments should take another look at the safeguard provisions and adjustment issues as they negotiate on subsidies. The FTA's ability to insulate Canadian producers effectively from U.S. protectionist pressures will greatly affect Canadian perceptions of the FTA and the tone of the broader relationship.

SUSTAINING THE MOMENTUM

The two national governments have passed the legislation and created the internal institutions necessary to implement the FTA. Yet, these measures by themselves do not ensure the success of the agreement. The timetables for tariff reductions are in place and could be accelerated; however, liberalizing nontariff measures is every bit as important. With regard to these, many FTA provisions are general and untested, and, as noted above, many provide only a standstill with the promise of future progress through negotiations.

For the FTA to work—specifically, to create an increasingly open environment for the flow of goods, services, and capital— the two governments must demonstrate that they will do the following:

- Abide by the spirit as well as the letter of the agreement.

- Make the dispute settlement mechanisms work.

- Devote the resources necessary to ensure the agreement's daily functioning.

- Address aggressively the ambitious negotiating agenda the FTA establishes.

- Renegotiate crucial segments of the agreement as flaws and problems become apparent.

Implementing the Agreement

As regards the first three points, adjusting to the disciplines of a comprehensive trade agreement will not be easy, and neither side can be expected to establish a perfect record. Minor aberrations and lapses will occur, giving rise to disputes and disappointments: too many political sensitivities and sensibilities about sovereignty are at play for this not to happen. One hopes, though, that such cases will have limited effect and duration as each side aggressively presses its rights under the FTA. Nevertheless, as indicated above, if the international economy experiences a prolonged recession or some other shock, U.S. and Canadian resolve to abide by the spirit of the agreement could be more rigorously tested.

This raises the familiar issue of the two "wild cards" in U.S.–Canadian relations—the Congress and the provinces. Will they, in every case, accept the constraints imposed by the FTA and quickly take action to respond to the findings of dispute settlement panels? On a more general level, Leyton-Brown brings to our attention the need to build public confidence among Canadians that the FTA constrains each country's actions equally. To this observation, the need to build similar confidence among members of Congress should be added.

Finally, this alerts us to the need for the United States not to regard the FTA as a done deal, but rather to devote the necessary resources and priorities to undertaking the complex tasks of day-to-day operations and continued negotiations. Assignments within the U.S. government are dispersed, raising serious questions about the administration's ability to maintain adequate focus and about the potential for bureaucratic rivalries.

The Negotiating Agenda

Leyton-Brown lists sixteen significant areas where the FTA mandates bilateral negotiations or other consultation and cooperation. These may be divided into five broad groups:[9]

- At the top of the list are the efforts to develop a substitute system of rules and disciplines for subsidies and dumping.

- The two governments have established a panel to study the future of the automobile industry; this could prove to be a precursor to other efforts at examining adjustment issues in specific industries.

- The governments will seek to harmonize, or at least make more compatible, a broad range of U.S. and Canadian policies, practices, and regulations. These include planned discussions to establish an open border for agricultural commodities and related products, and talks on product standards and technical regulations, business services and tourism, and financial deregulation.

- In other areas, raising similar harmonization issues, the two governments have, for now, agreed to seek progress mainly by cooperating in the GATT. These areas include government procurement, intellectual property, and agricultural subsidies.[10]

- Subjects will emerge that the negotiators did not anticipate—the oversights and flaws in the FTA that will become apparent as events unfold.

Harmonization Issues

Along with subsidies, the third and fourth groups are at the very core of modern trade negotiations. If, as Richardson asserts, subsidies, performance requirements, and unfair trade are the "hard bones of contention" in the current policy environment,[11] then harmonization to liberalize nontariff measures is the "flesh and muscle" of modern trade negotiations. Such harmonization often entails bridging significant, culturally based differences in national economic and legal institutions. Frequently, this confronts policymakers with difficult choices of whether to cede some power over particular levers of national economic and social policy or impede processes that could facilitate the freer flow of goods, improved competitiveness, and greater prosperity.

While all of the issues noted in the third and fourth categories above are being discussed in the Uruguay Round, the two governments have chosen agricultural regulations, product standards, and services as areas where they may be able to make more rapid or extensive progress on a bilateral basis. The real danger here is that some Canadians may interpret harmonization of U.S. and Canadian policies as compromising national sovereignty. Similar processes under the European Community (EC) 1992 initiative are tearing down nontariff barriers, giving producers in small European countries access to broader markets than currently enjoyed by Canadian firms. This could place Canadian firms at the same kinds of market access disadvantages with respect to nontariff barriers as they encountered a generation ago when the EC first removed tariffs. For Canada, the FTA is the means of addressing this challenge and achieving access to a market of comparable scope; it is not the primary impulse behind harmonization.

Subsidies, Adjustments, Safeguards, and Related Institutional Issues

As for the first, second, and fifth areas requiring bilateral cooperation, among the salient points of chapters 1 and 3 is that subsidies, adjustments, and safeguards are tightly intertwined issues. Richardson captures this nexus as he analyzes the consequences of domestic subsidies in the context of the increased international mobility of corporate capital:

> Mobility of large, multinational firms and their professional work force internationalizes ostensibly domestic policies. . . . Alert multinationals may decide that their expansion can be shifted to whichever of their affiliates enjoys the most favorable sectoral policy incentives. Technically "domestic" subsidies and taxes can thus easily become instruments of strategic sectoral predation among countries.[12]

Put another way, industrial policies, when strategically applied, can help shape a country's comparative advantage if they can move capital endowments and scarce technical expertise from one country to another through the mediating facilities of multinational firms. This process often leaves labor and other immobile resources behind, amplifying adjustment costs and increasing pressures for protection through safeguards, gray-area measures or whatever means may be at hand.

Although subsidies are at the top of the FTA negotiating agenda, U.S. and Canadian officials consider the safeguard and the related gray-area measures resolved issues in the bilateral context. However, Richardson, as noted above, perceives a danger that the FTA's global safeguard provisions may not insulate Canadian exporters when the United States employs VRAs; moreover, defining permissible Canadian market penetration when the United States seeks to include Canada in global safeguard actions could lead to the same kind of grudging negotiations that accompany the birth of VRAs. This is even more troublesome, given the difficulties governments encounter in providing degressive protection. Should such problems emerge, Canadians would feel deprived of important anticipated benefits under the FTA, and these issues would have to be resolved.

Turning to related institutional issues, Leyton-Brown alerts us to some of the FTA's potential shortcomings. These include the difficulties a *two-party* trade commission may encounter reaching consensus decisions in what are often perceived to be zero-sum situations and the trade commission's lack of a secretariat or single repository of records, precedents, and experience.[13] In addressing the subsidies and safeguard issues, Gary Horlick and Debra Steger, and Richardson, offer constructive suggestions along these lines.

The United States and Canada are not likely to forsake subsidies completely, nor are they likely to agree completely on which practices should be disciplined, either with each other or with other trading partners. Horlick and Steger's proposal is promising, because it would build on what the two governments may be able to agree to and recognizes the limits on what can be achieved bilaterally. Briefly, they recommend establishing structure, or committee, composed of officials from the two governments, that would review proposed and existing programs against lists of prohibited and permissible subsidies. For practices found to be in the prohibited category, or direct subsidies falling in the middle ground above x percent,[14] border measures similar to countervailing duties would be permitted without an injury test if the practice was not removed.[15] For indirect subsidies falling in the middle ground, countervailing duties would be permitted but a more rigorous injury test than currently applied would be required.[16] At least initially, the prohibited and permissible lists would be short, including items such as clear export subsidies, on the one hand, and social programs and health care, on the other.

This proposal has the virtue of permitting the United States to achieve some discipline on Canadian subsidies, while permitting Canada to maintain some limited flexibility to continue transparent and reasonably moderate regional and industrial aids (that is, direct aid below x percent) and a safe harbor for its social programs. Since regional and industrial aids are believed to be more prevalent in Canada, this proposal would give Canada something in return for the industrial benefits created by U.S. defense programs and provide the United States with a solution to the "five-to-one problem."[17]

With regard to safeguards, Richardson suggests redefining "domestic producers" eligible for temporary protection to include only workers, small firms, and other immobile resources, and establishing a permanent committee—an arms-length agent—to monitor and help manage bilateral safeguard actions. When either country considered a safeguard action following a determination of material injury, the committee could analyze alternative relief measures; when one government notified the other of its intention to implement a safeguard action, the committee could analyze the proposed action and, if requested, provide advisory opinions to aid the consultations required by article 1102.[18] Such a committee could provide the external discipline necessary for the two governments to resist permanent protection and to rely more on positive measures, such as small-business reorientation, severance bonuses for workers, and subsidies for retraining and relocation.

It is easy to see benefits to industry that are intended to ensure degressive protection and positive adjustment—for example, programs to encourage smaller but more modern competitors, and incentives to attract new employers to trade-impacted communities—becoming entwined with a discipline for subsidies. However, such temporary subsidies may prove less disruptive than safeguard actions and more effective in promoting adjustment. In the end, it may prove useful to combine the functions of the committees proposed by Horlick and Steger to deal with subsidies and by Richardson to deal with safeguards and adjustments. This committee could be supported by a group of designated technical experts from the two countries. In addition to dealing with problems as they emerged, the committee could be asked to examine adjustment issues in industries selected by the trade commission or the committee itself. If the committee could identify problem areas before they arose, bilateral approaches to adjustment might evolve. With so many industries organized on a binational basis (for example, automobiles) or engaged in fierce intraregional rivalries (for example, the New England–Atlantic Canada fisheries), which give rise to "hot" industrial and regional adjustment/promotion/predation disputes, such a process of joint study makes sense for avoiding conflicts and crafting mutually supportive, as opposed to competitive, public policies.

THE FTA AND THE GATT SYSTEM

The Uruguay Round marks a critical juncture for the GATT system. Slower growth in the industrialized countries over the past two decades and the increased number and range of development characteristics of participants in the GATT have magnified the adjustment challenges posed by new technologies, shifts in comparative advantages, macroeconomic imbalances, and sovereign debt problems. The proliferation of safeguard and gray-area actions is one important indicator of the difficulties industrial-country governments are encountering in maintaining public support for open markets and further multilateral liberalization. Moreover, the increasing importance of nontariff issues that require harmonization or greater compatibility among national policies, practices, and regulations greatly complicates the process of framing effective trade agreements. In this regard, difficulties emerge from national differences in approach and rigor for pursuing comparable goals—for example, product standards to ensure health and safety, and professional licensing to ensure the integrity of services providers. More perplexing, they also stem from significant national differences in views about what should be the overall goals of public policies—for example, intellectual property issues, such as patent protection and licensing for drugs—and about the appropriate scope of issues on the GATT agenda—for example, should labor flows be part of a comprehensive service framework? Together, these factors combine to make meaningful multilateral liberalization difficult and slow. Regional and bilateral agreements thus become attractive to policymakers, but dangers lie in carrying this approach too far.

Political leaders are attracted to regional and bilateral arrangements because such arrangements provide some of the economic benefits of broader multilateral progress, may entail fewer painful adjustments, and generally are easier to negotiate. Among smaller groups of countries having much in common in terms of development characteristics, economic and legal institutions, and political culture, the balance of economic benefits and adjustment costs is more predictable and controllable, and the technical problems of policy harmonization coincident with many nontariff issues are more manageable. Although the FTA may have its genesis in Canadian concerns about U.S. protectionism, and the 1992 program may have its origins in European fears of lost competitive viability, the practical realization of these ambitious initiatives owes much to the above-mentioned calculus.

Some public and private sector leaders have expressed interest in other bilateral partners for the United States; among those frequently mentioned are Japan, the East Asian newly industrializing countries (NICs), the Association of Southeast Asian Nations, and Mexico. None have as much in common with the United States as Canada in terms of their economic and legal institutions and approaches to policy; agreements comparable in scope and depth to the FTA are therefore unlikely. However, considering trade, capital, and labor flows, the U.S. and Mexican economies are already substantially integrated, and the two governments have strong incentives to find ways to bridge differences in their institutions and policies.[19] As Sidney Weintraub concludes, although Mexico is unlikely to see itself as part of the free trade movement in North America for now, the pressures on it to join in a wider North American arrangement will grow over time.[20]

FTA rules of origin notwithstanding, Canada would have an important stake in whatever agreements the United States negotiates with Mexico. For example, further integration of Mexico's inexpensive wage base into the cost structures of U.S. firms would reduce Canadian competitiveness in the U.S. market, and Canada might find that its interests are best served by active participation in an agreement.

Preferential arrangements can contribute to broader multilateral progress when they help make regional economies more integrated and efficient, and thus better prepared to adjust to multilateral liberalization; they are consistent with GATT principles and address issues in ways that are compatible with future progress in the GATT; and they do not create structures of bilateral/plurilateral preferences and benefits that, if upset, would engender resistance to future multilateral progress.

The FTA stands up well in these regards. It should strengthen the competitive capabilities of North American industry; its provisions are broadly consistent with GATT principles; its negotiating agenda is generally complementary to the Uruguay Round in both objectives and approaches; and it does not create disincentives for U.S. or Canadian participation in multilateral liberalization. The EC 1992 process, while improving the competitive viability of European industry, raises issues about discrimination and taxes Europe's capacity for adjustment, perhaps to the point of precluding for now meaningful multilateral progress.

A Mexico–U.S. or Mexico–U.S./Canada process of gradual liberalization, structured to be consistent with the FTA, though less rigorous and ambitious, could meet these requirements. However, the question remains whether increased competition from Mexico in mature industries would generate new pressures to limit U.S. and Canadian imports from other NICs and developing countries. Such an outcome would constrain U.S. ability to make concessions in multilateral trade negotiations to NICs other than Mexico and to developing countries, and would reduce U.S. prospects for achieving progress in areas such as services, intellectual property rights, and investment.[21]

This brings us to the general problems and real dangers that a proliferation of bilateral and regional agreements could pose. One is the recontracting problem, as successive agreements frustrate the expectations of preferential access engendered by previous agreements. Approaches to nontariff issues could vary with the business and legal traditions, cultures, and bilateral frictions. Although the United States is careful to standardize its bilateral approaches on specific issues,[22] arrangements with NICs and other developing countries centered on the United States, the EC, and Japan would almost certainly vary in their approaches. Taken together, these could impose large impediments to future multilateral progress. In the end, it may not be possible to build up a workable set of multilateral rules from a collection of bilateral and regional agreements.

A Mexico–U.S. or Mexico–U.S./Canada agreement that envisions Mexico's gradually increasing participation in an FTA-compatible arrangement could avoid this pitfall. However, a series of individual bilateral agreements with Asian and other Latin American countries could easily create obstacles to multilateral progress. Similarly, separate U.S. or Canadian participation in a series of bilateral arrangements could limit bilateral progress under the FTA.[23]

All of this argues for the United States and Canada to cooperate closely and proceed cautiously with regard to other bilateral initiatives. More fundamentally, it indicates that while recognizing that the FTA offers both countries important opportunities for North American economic progress, they should continue to look to the GATT as the most appropriate and primary vehicle for achieving broader progress and for opening markets and opportunities outside North America.

The FTA, like other emerging and expanding regional arrangements, was conceived as a response to the changing nature of international competition and the difficulties of achieving multilateral liberalization. The challenge for the United States and Canada is to use the FTA to positive effect by accepting its disciplines and tackling difficult problems—such as subsidies, safeguards, nontariff measures, and services—in a manner that both encourages positive adjustment and is consistent with future GATT progress. This will require political courage. However, it would strengthen the global competitiveness of the two economies and ensure that in North America, regional integration is a positive force for change in the broader multilateral system.

NOTES

1. For example, pharmaceutical patent protection, copyright protection for television signals retransmitted via satellite, and improved access for U.S. wine and spirits. See chapter 1, note 22.
2. Chapter 2, p. 27.
3. Chapter 3, Table 1, p. 62.
4. Chapter 3, pp. 68–69.
5. Chapter 3, Table 1, p. 62.
6. See Peter Morici, "The Canada–U.S. Free Trade Agreement," *International Trade Journal* (Summer 1988).
7. Labor market adjustments induced by free trade will likely be modest when compared with adjustments imposed by other shocks to the Canadian economy. See Ronald J. Wonnacott and Roderick Hill, *Canadian and U.S. Adjustment Policies in a Bilateral Trade Agreement* (Toronto and Washington, D.C.: Canadian-American Committee, 1987).
8. A. Jean de Grandpre, *Adjusting to Win, Report of the Advisory Committee to the Government of Canada on Adjustment* (Ottawa: Ministry of Supply and Services, 1989). See, for instance, chapter 3, p. 61.
9. Chapter 2, pp. 43–44.
10. In addition to these, Leyton-Brown lists a number of areas where the two governments will be reviewing progress with regard to specific commitments and technical aspects of the agreement—for example, customs valuation, temporary entry of business personnel, and broadcast retransmission rights. The FTA requires many other areas of discussion, but these are the principal ones.
11. Chapter 3, pp. 70–71.
12. Ibid.
13. Chapter 2, pp. 36–38.
14. The percentage would be a proportion of operating costs or capital, to be determined through negotiations.
15. In setting the rate of duty, consideration would be given to the import-substitution effects of the practice in the subsidizing country and third-country effects. In an integrated U.S.–Canadian market, 90 percent of the market for many Canadian, as well as U.S. producers will be in the United States; therefore, consideration of import substitution should provide more symmetry from a Canadian perspective.
16. Horlick and Steger make several recommendations to reduce the incidence and cost of countervailing duty cases, including consultations prior to initiating investigations; requiring a bilateral committee to determine

the sufficiency of evidence and a binational panel to provide an advisory opinion on the effects of a subsidy at the outset of an investigation and more rigorous standing requirements and definitions of injury. See chapter 4, pp. 91–92 and 93–95.

17. Chapter 4, p. 95, and chapter 6, pp. 132–133.
18. Chapter 3, pp. 74–76.
19. As discussed in chapter 6, the United States cannot significantly resist or redirect the pressures created by industrialization and lower wages in Mexico; it must accept Mexican goods, or continued immigration pressures, or both. For Mexico, the success of its economic reforms will require ever-increasing access to the U.S. market for its manufactures; diversion of U.S. markets from Mexican to Canadian suppliers as a result of FTA preferences, coupled with concerns about future U.S. trade actions, could inspire greater Mexican interest in a broad trade agreement with the United States.
20. Chapter 5, p. 120.
21. Ibid.
22. Consider, for example, the bilateral investment treaty program.
23. See chapter 6, pp. 146–148.

APPENDIX

The Steering Committee:
The Council on Foreign Relations International Trade Project

Edmund T. Pratt, Jr., Chairman
C. Michael Aho, Director of Project
Alison M. von Klemperer, Assistant Director of Project

Thomas O. Bayard
C. Fred Bergsten
Bill Bradley
William H. Branson
Sol Chick Chaikin
Lindley Clark
Ann Crittenden
June V. Cross
William Diebold, Jr.
William D. Eberle
Geza Feketekuty
Martin S. Feldstein
Murray H. Finley
Orville L. Freeman
Richard N. Gardner
Victor Gotbaum
Joseph A. Greenwald
Catherine Gwin
Robert D. Hormats
Gary C. Hufbauer
John H. Jackson
Abraham Katz
Harald B. Malmgren
Irene W. Meister

George R. Melloan
Ruben F. Mettler
John R. Opel
Sylvia Ostry
William R. Pearce
John R. Petty
Richard R. Rivers
Nicholas X. Rizopoulos
Felix G. Rohatyn
Howard D. Samuel
Daniel A. Sharp
Ronald K. Shelp
Leonard Silk
Joan E. Spero
Helena Stalson
John J. Stremlau
Peter Tarnoff
William N. Walker
Marina v.N. Whitman
Lynn R. Williams
Alan Wm. Wolff
Lewis H. Young
John Zysman

INDEX

Adjustments, 41, 133; arms-length
  agent and, 74–76; bilateral cooperation and, 165–66; bilateral
  pressures and, 61–66, 72, 75;
  Canada and, 158–60; corporate
  capital mobility and, 61, 70–72;
  distressed industries and, 134;
  domestic producers and, 72–74;
  employment and, 65–66, 67, 72;
  exchange rate and, 7; FTA and,
  1, 21; global pressures and, 66,
  67; Mexican–U.S., 147; pressure
  sources and, 60–61; safeguards
  and generalized, 667–68; safeguards and general overview of
  problems with, 68, 70; tariff abolition and, 61–64; U.S. and,
  157–58
Advertising, 51
Advisory Committee on Trade Negotiations, 41
Agricultural subsidies, 44, 55; countervailing duties and, 85; *see also*
  Subsidies
Agriculture, 10, 11, 15, 39, 43; adjustment and employment in, 65;
  Canada and, 5; U.S. and, 3, 129,
  136–37
Arms-length agent, 74–76
Auction quotas, 73
Australian–New Zealand Agreement, 125, 126, 140, 141
Automotive industry, 5, 16, 39, 43,
  111, 114, 116, 126, 131, 137,
  138, 143, 144, 149, 162
Automotive products, 4, 5, 9, 17

Baker, James, 34
Balance of payments (Mexico), 107
Banking, 17–18, 127; *see also* Financial services
Bilateral adjustment pressures,
  61–66, 72, 75. *See also* Adjustments

Bilateral agreements, 11, 15, 124,
  125, 133, 136; adjustment and,
  157–60, 165–66; Canada and,
  158–60; FTA and, 155, 156, 157,
  163–66, 167, 169; GATT and,
  140, 141, 144–48; institutional
  mechanisms and, 36–39; Mexican–U.S., 106; safeguards and,
  157; subsidies and, 163–66; U.S.
  trade policy and, 138–39,
  141–44, 149, 157–58
Binational review (subsidies), 91, 93
Brazil, 3
Broadcasting dispute, 51–52
Brown, Drusilla, 61, 64, 65
Budget deficit, 6–7, 55
Business, implementation and,
  40–42
Business services, 18

Canada: agriculture and, 5; exports
  and, 5–6, 7, 13, 14, 16, 21, 137,
  139; FTA objectives and, 13–15;
  GATT and, 55–56; implementation and, 30–31, 34–36, 55–56;
  imports into U.S. and, 109; investment and, 13, 17, 18, 138,
  149; macroeconomic constraints
  and, 7; manufacturing and, 6, 13,
  14, 158–59; market integration
  and, 155; Mexico and, 143–44,
  147; motives for entering FTA
  and, 2; protectionism and, 109;
  safeguards and, 137, 138; trade
  similarities and differences with
  Mexico and, 109–10
Canada–United States Trade Commission, 19, 157; implementation
  analysis and, 36–39, 45
Canadian International Trade Tribunal (CITT), 93, 94
Capital mobility, 61, 70–72, 163
Certification, 18
China, 3

175

ABOUT THE AUTHORS

Peter Morici joined the University of Maine in July 1988 as an associate professor of economics and Canadian studies, and is currently active with the National Planning Association as an adjunct senior fellow. He is also an adjunct member of the faculty at the School of Management, University of Massachusetts; a senior fellow at the Institute for Canada–U.S. Business Studies at Pace University; an adjunct fellow at the Center for Strategic and International Studies in Washington; a councillor of the Atlantic Council; and vice president of the North American Economics and Finance Association. From 1985 to 1989 he served as secretary-treasurer of the Association for Canadian Studies in the United States. His most recent publication is *Reassessing American Competitiveness*.

David Leyton-Brown is professor of political science, associate dean of Graduate Studies, and associate director of the Centre for International and Strategic Studies at York University in Toronto, Canada. Formerly a professor at Carleton University, he is the author of *Weathering the Storm: Canadian–U.S. Relations, 1980–83*, and editor of *The Utility of International Economic Sanctions* and *Trade-Offs On Free Trade: The Canada–U.S. Free Trade Agreement*.

J. David Richardson is professor of economics at the University of Wisconsin, and has taught at Wheaton College, the University of Michigan, and the Foreign Service Institute of the U.S. Department of State. He is a research associate of the National Bureau of Economic Research, and has been a visiting scholar at the Board of Governors of the Federal Reserve System and a consultant to the Economic Council of Canada.

Gary N. Horlick is a partner in the Washington, D.C., office of the law firm of O'Melveny & Myers, specializing in international trade and business services. He has served as international trade counsel for the U.S. Senate Finance Committee, deputy assistant secretary for import administration of the U.S. Department of Commerce, and as counsel to the Canadian government during the negotiations of the Canada–U.S. Free Trade Agreement. He has also taught international trade law at Yale Law School and Georgetown University Law Center.

Debra P. Steger practices international trade and competition law with Fraser & Beatty in Ottawa, Canada. She is currently on executive interchange with the Department of External Affairs and International Trade as a negotiator and coordinator in the Uruguay Round of multilateral trade negotiations. She is also an adjunct professor at the University of Ottawa Faculty of Law. Ms. Steger has written and edited several books and articles on international trade policy and law, including *A Concise Guide to the Canada–U.S. Free Trade Agreement* and *Understanding the Free Trade Agreement.*

Sidney Weintraub is the Dean Rusk professor at the Lyndon B. Johnson School of Public Affairs, University of Texas at Austin. Professor Weintraub testified before the Standing Committee on Foreign Affairs of the Canadian Senate prior to the decision to seek a free trade agreement with the United States, and he consults regularly with Mexican authorities on that country's trade relations with the United States. He is the author of many books and articles on U.S. trade relations with Mexico and Canada, including most recently one on Mexico, *A Marriage of Convenience.*